Beyond Blessed Parenting

Bill~
Blessings,

Psalm 91:4,

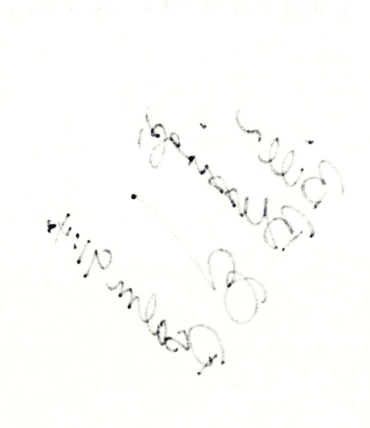

Beyond Blessed Parenting

Embrace These Seven Principles and Experience Authentic Connection

Tricia Thornton

Fitting Words

Nashville, Tennessee

Important Note from the Author:

Although I am a Licensed Professional Counselor (LPC) and a Registered Play Therapist (RPT) by profession, I am not *your* personal professional counselor or play therapist. All content and information in this book is for informational and educational purposes only, does not constitute health advice, and does not establish any kind of professional relationship by your use of this book. Although I strive to provide accurate general information, the information presented here is not a substitute for any kind of professional therapy or counseling, and you should not rely solely on this information. Always consult a professional in the area of your particular needs and circumstances prior to making any health decisions, be they physical or mental.

Publishing services provided by Fitting Words, LLC:

www.fittingwords.net

Print and ebook layout by Brian Kannard. bk@briankannard.com

ISBN: 978-1-5710248-9-3

Printed in the United States of America

1 2 3 4 5 6 7 8 9 10

For my dear husband, Jim,
and my two precious daughters,
Molly and Mary Evelyn.

For the brave reader to embrace,
even in the face of fear,
an authentic connection with God,
within, and with others.

What people are saying about
Beyond Blessed Parenting

I have practiced pediatrics for thirty years and recognize that it is much harder to be a parent today than in previous generations. In *Beyond Blessed Parenting*, Tricia Thornton walks through seven biblically grounded principles that can help parents in this age of social media perfectionism. Much like a flight attendant instructing you to put on your oxygen mask first, Tricia reminds parents to focus on their own mental health so they will be more equipped to care for their children.

Chetan R. Mukundan, MD

Beyond Blessed Parenting has a balance of psychological theory, research findings, practical suggestions for addressing issues such as fear and anxiety, and references to sources of spiritual guidance. Through the cases, Tricia Thornton covers a range of issues parents face in their everyday. Her own experience creates conversation with the reader.

Robert B. Innes,
Professor Emeritus, Peabody College at Vanderbilt University

Tricia Thornton's second book, *Beyond Blessed Parenting*, addressing the growing mental health crisis in this country, is a critical addition to the literature on this issue. Her book is real in its approach to a complex subject, truly a guide for parents searching for the best ways to navigate raising children in a world that seems to resonate more with chaos than with order. The stakes couldn't be any higher for our future, and this book is indeed a blessing for parents.

William R. Mott, PhD

With wisdom and care that has been gathered from years of careful parenting and the labors of a skilled therapist, Tricia Thornton shows us how to think about the importance of self-awareness and self-care in the very selfless task of being a parent. *Beyond Blessed Parenting* offers critical insights into the growing field of neurobiology and trauma, all framed in practical case vignettes and biblical insights that will benefit every parent in these complex times. We would all do well to take advantage of this resource.

Jason Brown, MA, LPC-MHSP

Table of Contents

Acknowledgments

This book is the product of many years in the making through my life experience, my marriage, parenting my two children, and years as a professional therapist. There are too many people to individually name, but I do want to specifically acknowledge some who have walked beside and supported me throughout this journey.

Jim, my husband, who stands strong and steady, always cheering me on.

Mary Evelyn, my older daughter, and Molly, my younger daughter, who always gave me hugs and encouragement even when I was away on my solo writing retreats. Allie, who still is greeting me every day at the door ready to selflessly love me with wagging her tail. Thank you to each of you for filling my bucket!

Susan, my older sister, who guided me in countless ways as I continue on this adventure.

—Tricia Thornton—

Mom and Dad, who both have shaped my parenting through mountains and valleys.

Dan Wright, my wise publisher (Fitting Words), and his team for the cheers and expertise and guidance.

Kate Etue, my gifted editor, who helped make this book one that many will embrace.

Lynn McCain and Benita Teems with McCain & Co. Public Relations for helping me to share this work with others.

Many friends, family, and colleagues who have walked through various stages of this journey. Each of you know, how much you have meant to me: Jill Rogers, Joanne Thornton, Anne Sineath, Ann Poteet, Anita Kay Hall, Anne Wooten, Bob Innes, Jason Brown, Chetan Mukundan, Bill Mott, Steve Johnson, Susan Mackey, Kelsi Ray, Trudy Waters, Ken Cheeseman, Harrison Taylor, Jamie Langley, Ashley Colclasure, Chap Clark, and my dear tennis ladies.

To all my clients who have bravely walked through the door of Tricia Thornton Therapy.

Preface

I am often asked, "What is the reason for the rise in mental health issues?" My answer invokes a bit of a surprised reaction. The increase in mental health issues is because parents have a difficult time prioritizing taking care of themselves. Another similar question I get asked from audiences, my clients, and other professionals is: "What is the most important thing parents can do?" The most important part of parenting is to prioritize self-care. We live in a world that is being driven by performance and busyness. Children's addiction to devices is often discussed and blamed for the rise in anxiety and depression. Indeed, children are too dependent on social media and technology. However, I feel, in general, that parents are more reliant on social media and technology than even their children. Yes, children need to play more and spend more time in nature. What I am saying is so do parents. I know this because I am a parent, and I reach for my phone too often as an escape and a way to numb fear.

—Tricia Thornton—

Take a minute to pat yourself on the back. You are choosing to take care of yourself by slowing down enough to read this book. Giving yourself a high five or a hug is hard, so know I am cheering for you. Parenting is not easy. Being a parent, whether of a newborn or adult children, is one of life's most challenging and draining experiences. We all feel the strain of ensuring we are empowering enough and not enabling our children. It is a constant battle of balance. After years of working as a therapist with children of all ages, I have realized the family system's foundation must be addressed. My prayer is that when you finish reading this book, you will not only walk away with tools in your parent toolbox but also, more importantly, discover that your own emotional bucket is a bit fuller.

You will see the word *connection* throughout this book. In my personal journey as a parent and from walking alongside many parent clients, I have concluded that to be a loving, present, and empowering parent, we must explore the idea of authentic connection. This starts with our relationship with God as we lean on His guidance to direct our paths. Then we are strengthened internally to connect with ourselves. From that connected place, we can parent and authentically connect with our children.

From one weary parent to another, let's go forward and learn together how to embrace the mountains and valleys of parenting. We will laugh, cry, doubt, and cling to the truth as we learn to parent ourselves. Here we go . . .

God

Oneself

With a Partner

Children

Cross of Connection

Introduction

I have set the stage. My candle is lit, a fresh notepad is positioned, and my instrumental worship playlist lightly hums. *Am I really ready? God, You have laid it on my heart to write book 2.* I don't feel the ink on *Blessing From Fear* has been dry long. In the depths of my soul, I know, without a second thought, this path has been set before me. However, the doubts pour into my consciousness: *How can I write a how-to parenting book? What if everyone figures out I am not a perfect parent? The world is in such a state of flux; how can this small book really help?* I name the fears. I acknowledge the many big feelings that arise within my heart.

We are a few years past a worldwide pandemic, a couple of years following a school shooting in my community, and right in the middle of a tumultuous election season. The statistics about anxiety and depression are rampantly rising, especially among our children. Parents are feeling an immense amount of pressure.

Daily, in my private counseling practice, I see tears and hear fears gripping my clients from ages four years young to seventy-five years wise. I almost feel as if I don't have a choice but to share these words. By no means do I have all the answers. I have real-life experience as a mother of two daughters, now ages eighteen and twenty-one, and wife, whose twenty-five-year marriage has been tested. The mountains and valleys, paired with about fifteen years of professional therapy experience, have certainly provided me with ample material and stories to bestow upon you.

Whether you are expecting your first child or parenting adult children, this book will provide you with guidance wrapped by a loving hand. One of the most important lines in these pages is "There is no perfect parent." Please take a pause and allow your heart to feel the relief. Even if you could master all seven principles, you still would make mistakes. I encourage you to explore one or two of the seven more deeply. One way to start is to begin with chapter 1, because embracing silence is a foundational principle. Then you can go on through the chapters in order or pick a principle that resonates with you more at this time and read that chapter. Ultimately, all the principles are important to our journey of embracing authentic connection. By the end of reading *Beyond Blessed Parenting*, you'll have a fuller parenting toolbox. You will also have seen and heard yourself with more compassion, and prayerfully, you'll be closer to God.

Overview of the Seven Principles

Throughout the last few years, I have noticed issues within myself that my clients have also been presenting, although mine are wrapped in different wrapping papers. These experiences have birthed, for me, a framework of how to be an empowering and affirming parent. It is based on seven principles. The idea is for us as parents to incorporate these principles into our own lives, then parent from that connected place. The seven principles are not a playbook just for you in your role as a parent. Instead, I challenge you to delve into the seven principles as a guide to growing yourself as an individual. Then you'll be able to put the tools into practice as a parent. I carefully chose the order to reflect a deep dive into your soul.

Principle 1: Silence

"He says, 'Be still, and know that I am God; I will be exalted among the nations, I will be exalted in the earth'" (Psalm 46:10). Silence starts with a stillness of the soul. If you're like, *Well, I'll never master this one. She has no idea how loud my life is within and around me,* don't close the book quite yet. You may be surprised at how you can view this foundational principle. Calm is not the goal. It's about embracing a connectedness within.

Principle 2: Listening

"I listen carefully to what God the LORD is saying, for he speaks peace to his faithful people. But let them not return to their foolish ways" (Psalm 85:8 NLT). The key word in this verse is *shalom*, which is translated "peace." In Hebrew, *shalom* conveys a sense of wholeness. It does not mean "without conflict." Let that rest for a few minutes. Listening is about being open to receiving, not being without valleys. As parents, if we first remain open to hearing God, then ourselves, we will be able to hear our children.

Principle 3: Acknowledgment

"In all your ways acknowledge Him, and He shall direct your paths" (Proverbs 3:6 NKJV). Acknowledging God is affirming that He is all-knowing even in trials. Putting God first in our lives is key. Visualize an image of a cross. At the top of the cross is God. Then, the top arm of the cross is connecting with oneself. The horizontal part of the cross is the connection between partners. The bottom leg of the cross is parents connecting with their children. If we as parents put our children above ourselves and God, we will be spinning our wheels, ultimately leading to unrest within us and our homes. I fell into this trap and still often struggle in this area. With grace at the center, repairs can occur within and around us.

Principle 4: Renewal

"Do not conform to the pattern of this world, but be transformed by the renewing of your mind. Then you will be able to test and approve what God's will is—his good, pleasing and perfect will" (Romans 12:2). The Hebrew word for *renew* means "refresh." I think of this idea as refocusing or reframing. This is not easy to do for ourselves, and it is certainly not easy as parents when all we see around us are trials and tribulations, from natural disasters to violence in our schools. The act of renewing our minds is a gift God gave us that entails an understanding of our beautiful brains. The brain and the mind are interconnected. The brain is the physical organ that supports the mind, which encompasses thoughts and feelings. In Romans, when Paul implores us to renew our minds, he also is encouraging us to understand the structure and functions of the brain. Understanding the power of both will enrich the act of renewal.

Principle 5: Forgiveness

"Brothers and sisters, I do not consider myself yet to have taken hold of it. But one thing I do: Forgetting what is behind and straining toward what is ahead" (Philippians 3:13). Thank you to the apostle Paul for confirming that perfection is not the goal. Let me be very clear: I am not saying we have to forget our hurts and trauma from our past as if the pain is not real. Forgiveness is truly the trickiest of the seven, because it is often misinterpreted. Through writing *Blessing From Fear*, it became clear to me that my past fears were holding me back from moving forward. Forgiveness starts with ourselves and God, then we look outward at our relationships with others.

Principle 6: Balance

"I press on to reach the end of the race and receive the heavenly prize for which God, through Christ Jesus, is calling us" (Philippians

3:14 NLT). "Pressing on" refers to the idea of moving forward, yet we are called to a balanced life. When we keep our sights on God to guide us as we move through valleys filled with pressures, we model a holy balance for our children.

Principle 7: Embrace

"For we are God's masterpiece. He has created us anew in Christ Jesus, so we can do the good things he planned for us long ago" (Ephesians 2:10 NLT). We are each an artful image created by God as His children. As parents, we must embrace all parts of us, distinguishing between the lies our inner critics tell us. We will find the freedom to fully know there is no perfect parent. Understanding the truths versus the lies will free us to embrace our children.

Meet the Characters

Throughout these pages, you will be privileged to get to know some relatable people. Each of these characters is fictional. Their journeys are made of bits and pieces of my life and my professional interactions over the years. From being in public and private schools as a school counselor to my practice as a Licensed Professional Counselor and a Registered Play Therapist, I have had the honor of walking alongside many people of all ages. Each of these individuals has real-life struggles and joys. I list each of the characters' primary fear responses. We all experience fear throughout our lives. Our brains were naturally designed to react to real or perceived fear in particular ways. The four fear responses are fight, freeze, flee, and fawn. I outline the four primary fear responses in more depth in the first chapter. Ideally, we want to intertwine all seven principles, but each person concentrates on one. Fear drives many big feelings to consciousness. You will get to see how each of the characters' fears ignites a response. You will get a bird's-eye view of my therapy sessions as I listen and guide each to use tools to incorporate their principles. Enjoy reading a brief overview of each of your new friends.

Sally

Sally is thirty-six years old and a mom of four children. She grew up in a family of five as the middle child. She struggles with a very busy life as a wife, mother, and caretaker of her aging parents. Sally needs to go back to work, so that is an added stress weighing on her. Slowing down to be silent evokes a palpable fear within her, prompting Sally's fawn fear response to surface.

Lawson

Lawson is a forty-two-year-old investing entrepreneur. He and his wife are raising two middle school–age sons and one elementary-age daughter. Lawson grew up in a very structured home. He often did not feel he could live up to the expectations of his politician father. Listening is not a known and accepted practice; instead, it evokes a flee fear response.

Alexander

Alexander is a fifty-five-year-old father of two teenage daughters and one son in college. He has been married for twenty-two years and is a hedge fund manager. After his parents divorced, he found himself having to raise his brother. He tends to get down on himself and has a glass-half-empty outlook on life. His mentor and fatherlike coach passed away last year, which brings up a fear response of fleeing and freezing.

Rose

Rose is a grandmother of two granddaughters and one grandson. Her family was riddled with a violent trauma that has caused a ripple effect. She has found herself not only taking care of her grandchildren but their parents as well. At seventy-two years old, she wants to travel but feels held back. She always tries to bring harmony into her life, and often her fawn response is ignited.

Francine

Francine is forty-nine years old and a mother of two daughters, ages fourteen and sixteen. Francine is a survivor of childhood sexual abuse. She has been a single mom after she and her husband divorced when the girls were younger. She works as an administrative assistant at a law firm. She often replays struggles in her mind, which causes her fight fear response to surface.

Brooke

Brooke is thirty-two years old and has a one-year-old and a three-year-old. Her husband has ADHD and travels with his job as an insurance adjuster. She often sees how being a daughter of a pastor influences her adult life. Recently her one-year-old underwent some testing for a possible genetic heart issue, which has raised her freeze fear response. She knows she needs to incorporate movement and balance into her life, but she feels stuck.

Elizabeth

Elizabeth is fifty-one years old and has three adult children. Her only daughter is getting married in a year, and one of her sons will be working as a teacher. Her youngest son has struggled with addiction for a few years. Her husband works as an IT entrepreneur, and Elizabeth struggles to figure out her role in life. She has a bent toward artistic interests and is weighing her options for her future. She feels like she lives a life of lies, and she is plagued by past addictive behaviors, which brings her freeze and flee responses online.

The Structure of This Book

The book is laid out simply—each part focuses on one of the seven principles. The three chapters in each section give more neurological and spiritual insights, relatable stories from our characters' lives, and practical tools for us to use as individuals and parents. Each part ends with discussion questions and invites you to incorporate that principle into practice. Look for the "Brainy Tidbits" sections for information about our brilliant brains. The feather from *Blessing From Fear* has returned! It brings tears to my eyes to carry that gift into this book too. The "Feather for Your Day" sections are encouraging spiritual insights.

I like to think of us going on this journey together. My prayer is that you will not only walk away with insights and tools but also blessings and affirmations. Parenting today is like a walk on the beach. It's beautiful, yet waves crash all around you. Some moments are smooth like the sand after the water recedes. At other times it is sharp with fragments of broken shells. In the end, however, the sun always rises and sets, giving us a glorious, colorful sky.

Deep breaths in and out. Let's start together with a bit of silence.

Part 1
Silence

Our society is much more interested in information than wonder, in noise rather than silence. . . . And I feel that we need a lot more wonder and a lot more silence in our lives.

—Fred Rogers

The idea is to still ourselves, to draw ourselves back to the deeper life that flows beneath the surface of our days.

—Sue Monk Kidd, *When the Heart Waits*

Chapter 1

The Busy Life of Sally

Beep, beep, beep. The alarm on Sally's iPhone blares out. It's 5:45 a.m. It's the third day of school, and she already is starting to feel the weight of her growing to-do list. Does her child's school really have to send out what feels like ten emails a day? Multiplied by three school-age children, that's thirty emails!

She is startled awake and rolls out of bed when she hears her one-and-a-half-year-old son calling, "Mama, Mama!" She trips over the dog toys and says a few choice words to herself. Her husband is already up and on his computer, planning how he will be able to meet his boss's deadlines. She sees the stack of resume drafts and a book titled *How to Go Back to Work as a Mother* on the kitchen table; she left it there the night before. She stops for a second, holding the baby, and thinks, *Ugh, I've got to get that done!* She goes into "mom mode" to pack lunches, fill water bottles, grab the dance leotard out of the dryer, and dump some cereal in bowls and bagels on plates. Oh goodness, she put milk in the five-year-old's bowl instead of the seven-year-old's.

Now, the taxi driving begins. It's Thursday, so at least she'll have three hours to herself while the baby goes to Parent's Day Out. By 9:35 a.m., she realizes she has been up for almost four hours and is already exhausted. She drives home to finally start working on her resumes.

Ding! "Oh crap!" she exclaims. The reminder on her phone feels like she stepped on a sharp shell on a beach walk. She has to be at her mother's home in fifteen minutes to take her to her memory care doctor's appointment. Oh well—there go her hours of solitude.

After a long day of carpooling, watching a gymnastics class, trying to fix a decent dinner, getting her parents' medicines all organized, and at least saying hello to her husband, she finally plops into bed. An eerie silence settles into her mind. For a second, she remembers what she heard on that podcast and watched on Instagram about being still. The silence ends abruptly when she hears pitter-patter down the hallway as her five-year-old jumps into the bed and squeezes between her and her husband.

Chapter 2

Fears of Silence

From a young age, silence was never easy for me. My six-and-a-half-year-old brain was filled with noise from the tears after my grandmother's tragic death in our driveway and my mother's scream after seeing robbers in our home. If I slowed down and allowed stillness or quiet to surround me, fear seemed to barge in through the door like a bull in a china shop. Over time, it became clear to me that if I stayed busy and loud, the fears of the robbers returning would stay at bay.

I painfully relate to Sally's busyness. Even though my story is different, I understand her avoidance of slowing down. For me, silence was an invitation to fear. Fear had "become an imprinted pathway in my brain. This fear encompassed many facets of my life. It was like an invisible string woven through the nooks and crannies of my *self*, controlling me and even dictating my relationships, my career, and my faith at various times throughout my life."[1] What I discovered while writing *Blessing From Fear* was how much my parenting was filled with noise. If I slowed myself down as a young parent and allowed silence to fill my soul, my brain's natural responses to fear would take over.

For me, silence was an invitation to fear.

The Fear Responses

God wired your brain to naturally react when it feels something is not right around you. All day and all night, your brain cues for safety. The mammal responses will ignite if the brain senses it is unsafe, even emotionally. Sometimes, these reactions can be lifesaving, but at other times, our brains become confused by the emotional noise. When this confused reaction takes place, your brain will respond in one of four ways.

Fight

The fight response is the body's attempt to defend itself physically against a threat. The fight response raises our vibrational state, or energy level. It can look like us yelling, using our fists, or using manipulation or passive aggression to fight against the threat. Often our tone of voice speaks louder and "fights" more than our words.

Freeze

The freeze response causes a near-dissociative state in which we "check out" mentally and emotionally. It can mimic an animal playing dead. This may look like us scrolling on social media or binge-watching a show to avoid conflict. This response feels like we are frozen and cannot decide what to do next. That overwhelmed feeling then leads us to just do nothing but check out from reality.

Flee

The flee response occurs when a person literally or figuratively runs away from their issues. It may look like running to another activity to fill the silence, such as filling our calendars, constantly having the TV or music on in the background, or even turning to serious addictive behavior. Sometimes, deflecting can be a form of the flee response. Deflection occurs as a form of avoidance when an uncomfortable situation occurs. Examples of deflection are shifting blame or changing the subject. It is as if we flee from the discomfort by delving into another activity.

Fawn

The fawn response to a threat takes the role of a peacemaker or a busy helper. It might look like organizing a meal train, coming to the rescue, or helping to settle an argument between family or friends. In general, those who fawn want to take care of everyone but themselves. This response is hard to detect sometimes because it comes across as being helpful and nice.

My natural fear response is to fawn. Throughout childhood, I tried to be the peacemaker to deflect my parents' rocky relationship. Sally and I both get caught in the trap of busyness to avoid the fear that can arise if we dare to slow down. The unhealthy side of my fawn response began to put a wedge between me and my husband. Slowing down and connecting with him seemed scary and vulnerable, so the noise and negative messages became more familiar, leaving my brain in a state of busyness. After some concentrated efforts of self-awareness, I have learned not to allow the running to block the stillness that my soul longs for. Shortly, we will see how Sally learns to allow herself some silent solitude.

The Brain's Role in Silence

Before we get back to Sally, let's explore the principle of silence more deeply. Do you know that your brain has a network that houses the art of silence? Three different modes or networks of the brain involve various regions: the default mode network (DMN), the salience network (SN), and the task positive network (TPN). The SN is mainly responsible for recognizing stimuli. When you feel anxious or fearful because of stimulation around you, your SN is most active. As you're reading right now, your TPN

> ### *Brainy Tidbit*
> **The default mode network (DMN) is active when we are silent and still.**

is lighting up. This network is activated when you are engaged in a task, such as writing and reading. The DMN then becomes most active when you're in a resting state. When you are still and engaging in silence, your DMN is at work. However, when we finally slow down and our DMN is activated, our SN may quickly sense fear and switch our TPN on.

Spiritual Insights of Silence

You may be familiar with the story in Luke 10:38–42 about Mary and Martha. For the longest time, I did not find comfort in this story. I actually felt frustrated and even a bit attacked. In the story, Jesus and His disciples are traveling with their ministry. They stop by the home of two sisters, Mary and Martha. Martha's TPN is running around full of to-dos to prepare for a dinner party for Jesus and the disciples. Her sister, Mary, has her DMN awake and sits at the feet of Jesus, listening in silence.

Jesus looks at Martha and acknowledges that she feels worried and is upset. He tries to point Martha to put God first when He says, "Mary has chosen the better part, and it will not be taken away from her" (v. 42 NCB). I used to get irritated when I read this because I thought God was abandoning Martha and telling her that making her home nice and pretty was not the "Christian" thing to do. That is a lie that I was telling myself. I imagine Sally gets caught in a similar untruth. Martha and Sally may have believed they had to be busy, or they would feel unproductive and lazy. This trap was all too easy for me to fall into as a busy young parent. What we glean from this story is not that making your home inviting or setting an elegant table is bad; but if the busyness of these tasks fills the silence with noise, then that can lead to pure exhaustion and anger. Fear often causes us to run to busyness, but our brains cherish stillness.

Fear often causes us to run to busyness, but our brains cherish stillness.

Two of the most common feelings I hear from parents when they first come to see me are *weariness* and *resentment*. Their eyes fill with tears as they tell me they do not feel much joy in their lives. They relay that they have moments and glimpses of happiness, but overall, noise has filled the silence within their souls. Parenting is a journey full of mountains and valleys. It often feels that sometimes we take five steps forward and then two steps back. Daily, I have to remind myself that it is not about perfection but about connection. Let's find out ways we can invite some silence into our lives, so we can begin to authentically connect with God, ourselves, our partners, and then our children.

Feather for Your Day

Silence is a form of prayer. Stillness is a way to say "I love you" to God.

Chapter 3

Inviting Silence

Sally wakes up and realizes she has not really slept well in weeks. Her five-year-old is coming into their bed every night. She is at a loss because sleeping has not been an issue for their daughter for some time. She remembers her friend telling her about a child therapist who worked with their daughter. Exhausted and angry, she decides to give me a call.

In the initial intake phone call, I hear Sally's issues related to her five-year-old daughter. She also shares that her seven-year-old daughter seems to be showing signs of anxiety at the start of second grade. Her three-and-a-half-year-old son's meltdowns are becoming more frequent. The baby and her other child, thankfully, are easy for now. We decide to start our therapy with me working with Sally as a parent.

I often find if I can guide parents, the child may not even need to come in to see me, or the number of sessions may be reduced. I try to reassure Sally that she is giving herself and her family a gift by coming in. It takes courage to start to ask for help.

The Power of Co-Regulation

Have you ever walked into a room where you could feel the energy in the space? It feels like the room is buzzing and there is a lot of noise. It feels heavy and sometimes even a bit overwhelming. As we connected, Sally began to notice a pattern. When she was busy and feeling stressed, the noise level of her home would increase. As her energy rose, so did the energy of her children. This is due to the power of co-regulation.

Regulation is the ability to choose a healthy reaction in response to our big emotions. Children co-regulate off their caregivers, meaning they emulate their parents' emotions with their actions. This phenomenon occurs because of amazing neurological concepts.

Regulation is the ability to choose a healthy reaction in response to our big emotions.

Our brains have what are called mirror neurons. They are brain cells that activate when an individual performs an action or observes another's actions. God literally wired our brains to connect. These mirror neurons allow us to observe and mimic another's actions, emotions, and energy state. Most days, Sally felt she jumped from activity to activity. From answering emails whenever she had a moment to constantly picking up toys, organizing the house, and keeping up with the family calendar, she felt she was moving and doing all day. As Sally's busyness clouded her brain, her children subconsciously received a message that being busy equals success. Their brains stayed in a reactive state, causing hypervigilance. The behaviors that

were coming to the surface were disrupted sleep patterns, anxiety, and tantrums. The pressures in school and around the world were compounding the children's negative energy. Children do not yet have the brain circuitry to rationally communicate their overactive state, so they began to mirror Sally's busyness. Their overactive brains were causing them not to be able to regulate their emotions; therefore, they began to have more dysregulated behaviors. The negative behaviors looked like complaining, disobedience, whining, and frequent meltdowns. The truth is, even though we adults have the fully developed wiring, we sometimes do not react within reason as well!

Active Waiting vs. Passive Waiting

Waiting can be painful because we feel we aren't doing anything. Passive waiting means to sit back in an idle state, disengaged. Active waiting is to be present in the here and now. It is being aware of the five senses in the moment. That may be having an awareness of what is going on all around you on a sensory level. For example, even in the busyness of a day, you stop and notice a beautiful tree full of changing fall colors. Even while waiting in line at the grocery, pause and smell the flowers at the checkout counter. It requires engagement and connection within and with God. Remember our dear sisters, Mary and Martha? Mary practiced actively waiting as she sat at Jesus's feet and listened to Him. Martha got caught in the trap of believing that waiting was, in general, not productive. Today, Martha may have gotten confused and felt that scrolling TikTok would equal stillness, but that is actually passively waiting.

Sally often reported feeling that she was silent, lazy, or unproductive in her daily life. Her husband was a very hard worker and did not slow down much either. She grew up as a middle child with two older brothers and two younger sisters. There was always noise around her. Her brain really did not ever know what it meant to be still. When I shared this idea of active waiting versus passive waiting with her, she was intrigued but had not been convinced yet.

Feather for Your Day

God whispers to us in silence, just as He whispered to Elijah on the mountain after the earthquake (1 Kings 19:12). Can we emotionally hear His whispers?

Tools to Use to Invite Silence

After a few months of therapy, Sally was still reporting her children were not sleeping, were having anxiety, and were melting down more frequently, so we discussed a few tools she could be using herself to make small shifts at home. Sometimes, we think we must make drastic changes and undergo a complex overhaul of our family systems to see change. But in reality, slight movements can cause more substantial and lasting change. I recommend the following to invite silence into your soul as an individual and into your home as a parent.

Slight movements can cause more substantial and lasting change.

Use Mindful Grounding Exercises

Grounding involves being self-aware and using techniques to bring yourself to a regulated and balanced state. It ultimately leads to authentic connection. We will cover many grounding methods throughout this book, so choose the ones that fit well for you. Journaling, expressive art activities, and listening to calming music are useful methods to help you notice patterns of noise that come into your consciousness while trying to be silent. Journaling can take on several forms. Writing is just one way of recording your thoughts. Voice journaling is using your device to talk and text your thoughts into a notes app. When we can make space in our minds, we will be able to make room for silence to enter. Sometime, our thoughts cloud our brains, so we must make head space for the stillness.

Art can be effective as well. Sketch, paint, or color an image that represents your thoughts. Using photography can also work well to capture what the silence is telling you.

Music engages your auditory sense, which awakens the prefrontal cortex region of the brain. Some like to listen to instrumental music while some like to listen to more worship-filled songs.

Sally decided to try to use voice journaling because she spent a lot of time in her car. She would open her phone's notes app before leaving her driveway and just start talking, and the phone would record her thoughts. For many of us, alone time in the car will make our thoughts start flowing.

Be Silent in Small Doses

Sally and I figured out she mostly could be still and invite silence into her soul while driving to and from her kids' activities. Her youngest child typically was quiet or sleeping while in the car. That was not always the case with her three oldest children, but thankfully her fourth child was so used to going to and fro with Mom that he slept easily in his car seat. I suggested Sally try to make a point not to schedule any calls during the ten-minute ride to school to pick up the other children and instead, focus on silence.

Sometimes when we are learning how to be silent, it is easier to be "doing" something rather than simply sitting still. If driving isn't a great option for you, you could try taking a walk. Even folding laundry can be a monotonous activity that can invite silence. Try not turning on the TV while folding and just noticing the sounds of the birds outside. Leisurely riding a bike or slowly doing the elliptical can be relaxing, yet we are still moving our bodies. Light yoga is also a way to move, while still engaging in silence.

Instill an Alone Time into Your Family Routine

Alone time provides time away from anyone so an individual can regulate and become more self-aware. The overall premise is that each family member will have some alone time in their own space. The goal is to bring the energy level in your home down a notch or two to allow healthy co-regulation to occur. Time alone will help children and adults self-regulate. Children have to be "on" all day. They rarely have time to themselves to just "be" during their day, especially if they are in a traditional school setting. Having quiet alone time at home—whether you call it "me time," "creative time," "my time," or "alone time"—will empower a child to realize they have the ability within to ground themselves and choose a healthy reaction to big feelings.

There are a few dos and don'ts to be mindful of for the alone time to be successful. Make sure to not call it "time out" because that can have a negative connotation. The amount of time to spend alone depends on the age of the children. Ages three to five years old can be expected to be alone for about ten to fifteen minutes. Ages six to nine years old can handle twenty minutes, increasing up to thirty minutes for older children. If there are space constraints then just being in different corners of the room is okay. Start in opposite corners of the room if the child is having separation anxiety. They can see you but not interact with you. There is not to be any technology usage during alone time. I encourage that same rule for the parents as well.

The introduction of alone time is key. You'll want to present the idea to the family when all are pretty much grounded and happy. Possibly explain it over the weekend and then start the alone time the following school week. You can point out how busy all have been, and it would be a great idea for all to have some alone time. I like to point out to the siblings the positive side of not having their brother or sister bug them for a few minutes. You will want to pick a calming alarm sound to start and end the alone time. Be sure to review the options of activities that a child can do during their time, such as playing outside, dancing in their room, drawing, coloring, playing with kinetic sand, constructing with LEGO blocks, doing a craft, reading, or resting while listening to music.

After alone time is over, I often encourage families to have a bit of playtime or even a dance party to enjoy some fun together.

After a few weeks of trying out all these tools, Sally noticed some shifts within her. She was not feeling as angry and even felt a bit more energy. Her daughter was now coming to her bed only when there was a thunderstorm. Her older daughter was sharing that her anxiety was mostly about being in a new class at school. Sally began to treasure her ten-minute drive to school, and it became a sacred time for her to offer silent prayers to God. The family was still working out the kinks with the alone time, but she was seeing some of the benefits of each having individual time to reset. She did notice that when they made a point to follow the suggestions, the house overall seemed a bit calmer and more connected.

The Courage to Be Silent

Ecclesiastes exclaims, "There is a season for everything" (3:1 ISV). There is a "time to be silent and a time to speak" (v. 7). Courage is found in the stillness. Silence allows our souls a time of rest. Parenting is not about perfection but about connection. We as children of God were given brilliant brains that can choose silence so we can connect with the divine. There will be ups and downs, like riding the waves on the ocean. Sometimes, we find ourselves in the dip of the wave, and other times we coast on the wave's crest. Connection through silence can allow us to feel we can face the ups and downs of life with a bit more balance. When we first hear and see ourselves, we will then be able to empower and affirm our children through the silence within our souls.

***Parenting is not about perfection
but about connection.***

Journal and Reflection Questions

For Discussion

What noises fill your brain when you are trying to invite in silence?

_____

_____

_____

_____

What primary fear response awakens within you when you sense fear?

_____

_____

_____

_____

Which mindfulness activity will you embrace to invite moments of
silence into your life?

_____

_____

_____

_____

A Verse for Silence

"He says, 'Be still, and know that I am God; I will
be exalted among the nations, I will be exalted in
the earth.'"

Psalm 46:10

Part 2
Listening

I have to kneel before the Father, put my ear against his chest and listen, without interruption, to the heartbeat of God.

—Henri Nouwen, *The Return of the Prodigal Son*

We should listen with the ears of God that we may speak the Word of God.

—Dietrich Bonhoeffer, *Life Together*

Chapter 4

The Lost Life of Lawson

Lawson loves this time of year. It's April and his favorite professional golf tournament, the Masters, is set to begin soon. He's reminiscing about his college golf days as he finalizes the two-day trip to the iconic Augusta National Golf Club with his clients. As he walks out of his home office, he sees the picture of his father on the floor of the Senate and a quote that he heard often as a child: "Performance is the key to success." He notices a tense sensation in his chest and pauses, but that moment is interrupted by his thirteen-year-old son standing in front of him, waiting for affirmation of his art project. He hears his wife trying to separate his other two children after his seven-year-old destroyed her older brother's detailed LEGO city. Lawson catches himself before he yells, "Why can't everyone just listen to me!"

He remembers his son standing there and says to him, "Looks good, Son. Maybe add a few more colors to make it better." His son walks away, feeling dejected and not seen. Lawson feels that chest tension again. He walks into the kitchen and asks his sons to get their clothes on because it's time to head to the driving range. They both remind him they have to go to their art class and then a birthday party in thirty minutes. *Well*, he thinks, *they're certainly not like me!* He tells his wife he'll be back in two hours and walks out the door.

On the way to the range, he turns on the sports talk radio. He feels his knee tighten, and for a few minutes, he's right back to the day his injury changed the course of his life. He gets to the range and sees his good friend and pastor. He thinks, *I have not read that book about parenting. Ugh! My men's small group is on Tuesday before I leave for Augusta.* The strange tightness in his chest and neck occurs again. He gets out of the car to go greet his friend when he notices his friend's sons are with him. He grabs his clubs and walks alone toward the putting green instead.

Chapter 5

The Cross of Listening

Listening has not been easy for me. I feel I can relate to Lawson in this way. Ironically, God called me into the profession of a therapist because I have to hold space for my clients as their story keeper. To be present with my clients, I must first be attuned with God and with myself. Attunement occurs only when one is present in the here and now. You can be present and not attuned to someone, but you cannot be attuned without being present. That's a mouthful, so feel free to read that statement twice.

The Framework of the Cross of Connection

Affirming our children to be empowered to honor healthy choices occurs when we look at parenting from the framework of a cross. At the top is God. We must first be present and attuned in our relationship with God. Remember that does not mean perfection but connection. Whether through prayer, reading the Bible, singing, or fellowship, our connection with God comes first.

Then, we need to listen and tune into ourselves. Sally uses journaling as a way to connect within herself. I'll be going over other examples throughout this book, and you'll see that Lawson uses another tool.

Finally, connection between the two parents is key. You may have noticed in Lawson's story, no parent has connected with a child yet. Through my parent sessions, I help guide parents to attune with each other as they understand their love languages and attachment styles. After the top part of the cross is more balanced, then a parent can truly be present and attuned so authentic listening can occur. The balance of the cross of connection opens the path for listening.

The balance of the cross of connection opens the path for listening.

The Brain's Role in Listening

Listening involves being open and receiving. Four structures of the brain work together to allow us to be open to listening. The insula region acts like an internal awareness center, receiving information from the body's cues through the thalamus. The thalamus is like Grand Central Station, taking in messages from our five senses. The message then is sent to either the amygdala or the prefrontal cortex region. The amygdala, the emotional hub in the limbic region, assesses big feelings such as fear. To authentically listen, the message must be routed to the fourth part, the prefrontal cortex. This region houses the executive functions, such as regulation and organization. It is where we turn this sensory input from emotional reactions to log-

ical responses. But if the flow is interrupted, and the message gets stuck in the amygdala, then the individual cannot authentically listen because they become hypervigilant and reactive.

Spiritual Insights of Listening

Often, we get clouded by the noise from society. Whether it is from social media, the news, or our peers, our ability to listen becomes muffled as we feel pulled in a variety of directions. Jesus is the master listener. There are many places in Scripture where we can learn about listening. Two stand out in my mind. One is in John 4:4–42 when the Samaritan woman had been outcast, possibly for being barren, which made her not accepted in her culture. Jews did not interact with Samaritans, so the fact that Jesus stopped to intently be open and connect with this woman makes this story even more beautiful.

Another time Jesus listened to someone silenced by society is in Mark 10. Jesus was on the way to Jerusalem when he met a blind beggar named Bartimaeus. The man called out to Jesus for Him to take pity on him. Jesus powerfully told the crowd to be quiet so He could listen to the man.

In both of these stories, the two people He listened to were not perfect at all but shamed by society. I am often reminded that listening is about opening our hearts to hear first God, then ourselves, then others.

Feather for Your Day

Listening is about opening our senses to allow the Holy Spirit to guide us to hear Our Father as the master listener.

Chapter 6
Learning to Listen

Lawson returns from his trip to the Masters feeling tired and tense. He has an important week ahead as he is trying to close a deal with a new client. Before he leaves for the firm, his wife reminds him they have a therapy appointment later that day. He thinks, *Therapy?! Why are we going anyway? The kids are better now. We are okay. I mean, we aren't perfect, but we're fine. How much is this going to cost me anyway?* He half smiles at her and walks out the door. When he gets in the car, he notices the corner of the parenting book peeking out from his files on the passenger seat. He puts his coat over it and "flees" by listening to the chatter of yet another sports radio talk show.

Lawson and his wife's first session focuses a lot on their backgrounds and the results of their love language and attachment style quizzes. Lawson lights up as he talks about his younger golf days.

He notices my Masters cup sitting on the table and shows a smile of curiosity and connection. When I ask about his childhood, he looks a bit lost. He isn't sure how to answer. I take a bit of time explaining his and his wife's attachment styles. Lawson listens with interest but rubs his neck with persistence. Initially, it can be confusing for parents when we start with information about their own childhoods. To gain a fuller understanding of how the cross of connection is working in the family system, it is helpful to gain a fuller picture of one's own family of origin.

Understanding Attachment

John Bowlby, one of the early pioneers of attachment theory, taught that our fundamental relationships with our caregivers create a blueprint for our future connection. Then in the 1970s, Mary Ainsworth expanded on Bowlby's attachment work with her groundbreaking "Strange Situation" study. Through her research, three major attachment styles were derived: secure attachment, ambivalent-insecure (anxious) attachment, and avoidant-insecure (dismissive) attachment. A fourth style, disorganized-insecure attachment, was named in 1990.[2]

What you need to know is that the styles are formed early in the first year of life based on how the primary caregivers respond to the baby's cues. No one is fully secure or insecure; there is a continuum. I detail each style in chapter nine of *Blessing From Fear*.

Here is a brief description of each of the four styles:

Secure Attachment

The primary caregiver consistently met the infant's emotional and physical needs. An adult with this style feels safe, confident, and able to trust within themself and with others. It doesn't mean the securely attached individual will not experience pain and trauma, but they will be able to put healthy boundaries in place.

Ambivalent-Insecure (Anxious) Attachment

Other names for this style are "anxious-preoccupied," "ambivalent-anxious," or "anxious-ambivalent." This individual's primary caregiver did not consistently meet the infant's needs and was unavailable and distracted. That inconsistency led the individual to feel anxious. As an adult, this individual is often distracted by anxiety. There is a craving for closeness, but vulnerability and openness do not feel safe.

Avoidant-Insecure (Dismissive) Attachment

This individual is the opposite of the anxious person who craves intimacy. Because this person's caregiver often rejected their needs, this individual often avoids relational closeness. It's like they have built up a thick wall of protection around themselves. The distance between the infant and the caregiver caused this adult to create that same sense of self-reliance and avoidance of closeness.

Disorganized-Insecure Attachment

Another name for this style is "fearful-avoidant," which stems from the infant experiencing intense fear or trauma as a child. Often the caregiver was negatively parenting due to their unresolved trauma. This adult struggles to manage their big feelings, often resulting in trying to control others or falling into the trap of addictive behaviors.

Lawson's attachment style is most similar to avoidant-insecure (dismissive). His mother was caught up in the socialite world of marrying a highly revered politician. She often did not have time to meet Lawson's needs consistently. His father tried to steer Lawson toward politics, but he was always drawn to sports, in particular golf. In Lawson's childhood, performance was stressed as a measure of success. Under his tough exterior, Lawson desires closeness from his wife and children, but he does not know how to allow himself to trust that others will meet his emotional needs. He finds himself avoiding close relationships as a way to protect himself from feeling rejected and dismissed.

Brainy Tidbit

Attachment styles are formed from the brain's limbic region, the emotional center. Mirror neurons enable infants' brains to attach and connect with their caregivers' brains.

Tools to Use to Learn How to Listen

After a couple of parent sessions, we decided it would be helpful for Lawson to come in individually. In the first few sessions, Lawson slowly began to open up about what he felt he'd never heard in his home. He felt he was often dismissed by his wife and children, so he avoided too many interactions of closeness. Lately, he had begun to really desire to spend time with his children, but he struggled because he found they were so different from him. When he talked about his family and his family of origin, I noticed Lawson began to touch his chest and his neck. When I inquired about that, he shared he often felt tense. That was my cue to share with him some ways his body could help him heal his fears of getting close to others.

Five Senses

Recall the brain's insula retrieves inklings from the five senses through the thalamus. These messages then travel to either the amygdala in the limbic region or up to the prefrontal cortex, our executive center. I showed Lawson my brain model to visually guide him to an understanding of our brain's God-given power. If the five senses can neurologically help us to connect more to God and within ourselves and ultimately with others, why not use them with intention?

The five senses activity I teach is simple. Anytime and anywhere, ask yourself:

- "What are three things I see?"

- "What are three things I hear?"

- "What are three things I feel?"

- "What are three things I taste?"

- "What are three things I smell?"

If, after going through the senses, you don't feel connected within, then repeat the questions a few more times. By the way, for younger children, it is okay just to recall the first three senses: see, hear, and touch. It's also acceptable for adults to do the same.

Healing and regulation do not always look perfectly calm but connected. What I mean by this is that when someone is connected, they can still have emotions. We can even look nervous or fearful, but be aware of the big feelings and be able to choose a healthy reaction. We are connected by noticing and naming our feelings and then deciding what action we will take next.

Healing and regulation do not always look perfectly calm but connected.

Guided Imagery

There are many versions of guided imagery. The one I prefer to teach first uses the five senses. I asked Lawson to tell me about a time when he had felt peace, happiness, and connection within. He recalled walking on the grounds of his high school's golf club.

I guided him to close his eyes and picture walking onto the first tee. He visibly began to relax. I then proceeded to tell him to take three deep breaths. Then, I asked him what three things he could see as he was looking out at the tee. Then I asked what three things he could hear. Then what three things he would be touching. I kept guiding Lawson through all five senses. When we were done and after taking three more deep breaths, I invited him when he was ready to look back at me. He was amazed at how the tension in his neck and chest had lessened.

Body Scan Meditation (BSM)

To continue with being aware of your body's cues, I teach my clients to use a body scan meditation. When Lawson came in for his next session, he discussed his hard week with his clients. He also talked about a difficult conversation he had with his mother about his father's estate. His father passed away about six months prior. I asked if he would be okay with me guiding him through a body scan meditation. He was hesitant at first, but I told him many athletes use this form of relaxation often. He was a bit more open to the idea.

BSMs can take a few minutes up to a longer time period. It's up to your preference. There are several good online options. The Calm app has some I have personally enjoyed. Usually, the facilitator will start with the toes and work up to the head. You're focusing on each part and noticing any tension in each area. The body is a window into your soul and your mind. As Lawson began to unwind, he was able to connect with his feelings within and explore listening to God and to himself.

The Power of Listening

Authentically listening to another person starts with a connection first to God and then within yourself. As the cross is formed, parents will be able to see and hear their children. "To achieve soul harmony within our families, we must choose to embrace God's gift of neuroplasticity (the fact that our cells can change and interact) and epigenetics (the power of our brain to change our genetic makeup)."[3] We are all made in God's image. He made us able to attune within our bodies so our brains can cue us to be open and present and vulnerable to His guidance.

Feather for Your Day

Romans 12:2 guides us to "Not conform to the pattern of this world, but be transformed by the renewing of your mind," We have the power through the Holy Spirit to renew the state of our minds to be present and attuned with another.

—Beyond Blessed Parenting—

Journal and Reflection Questions

For Discussion

How do you connect with God, within yourself, with another, and with your children?

_____

_____

_____

_____

Which attachment style do you most identify with? How do you see that the style influences your parenting?

_____

_____

_____

_____

Where do you most sense big feelings within your body?

_____

_____

_____

_____

A Verse for Listening

"I listen carefully to what God the LORD is saying, for he speaks peace to his faithful people. But let them not return to their foolish ways."

Psalm 85:8 NLT

Part 3
Acknowledgment

Nearly all the wisdom we possess, that is to say, true and sound wisdom, consists of two parts: the knowledge of God and of ourselves. But, while joined by many bonds, which one precedes and brings forth the other is not easy to discern.

—John Calvin, *Institutes of the Christian Religion*

Acknowledge that the LORD is God! He made us, and we are his. We are his people, the sheep of his pasture.

Psalm 100:3 NLT

Chapter 7

The Unaffirmed Life of Alexander

Alexander looks at his watch. All is going like clockwork so far. He walked and fed the dog, turned on the Keurig, and started to fry two eggs, cooked some turkey sausage, and cut up a banana. He feels satisfied as he sits down for a peaceful moment.

That peace is short lived when his two daughters' morning rants start up. His oldest daughter is in a fury, looking for her volleyball uniform. His wife jumps in to try to keep the peace. He hears his daughter chirp, "Mom, help me! You always find it. It's a mom thing." The youngest is getting more and more exasperated and yells, "It is freezing! We are going to have to park in overflow! Come on!"

Alexander's well-orchestrated breakfast is getting colder by the moment. In the meantime, the aged goldendoodle grumbles at all the noise. Alexander looks at Sadie the dog with a sense of familiarity, as if he is having those exact thoughts himself. He has a fleeting realization that in just three and a half short years, he will have an empty nest. His son is already at college as a sophomore. He snaps back to and routinely kisses his wife before rushing out the door to his downtown office. He follows his girls out of the neighborhood and turns left as they turn right toward their high school. He mentally checks his to-do list before his 11:00 a.m. Zoom call with his California client.

All of a sudden, he gets cut off and he screams a few expletives at the car. He feels his blood pressure rise and becomes incensed at the amount of construction that makes him reroute. Once again, he gets a sense that time is flying by him like a feather blowing down the road.

Finally, he pulls into the parking garage. He walks up five flights of stairs to get in more daily steps. He puts his bag on the shelf, straightens his pens, turns on his computer, and opens his blinds. He quickly checks his email before his meeting starts.

He notices a message from a college friend announcing an upcoming reunion. A flood of thoughts rushes in. *Crap, do I have to go? I know they're having a dedication ceremony for Coach, so I have to be there. I think that means Julie has to join me too. I wonder if we can make it a family trip and make it fun? Fun, ugh, I have to . . .* A ding loudly interrupts his inner dialogue as the stock market's opening bell sounds.

After his busy day, he whisks off to the high school for his daughter's volleyball game. On his short way home, he gets a call from his college buddy asking him to speak at the dedication ceremony. Once again, the inner conversations start. After a fit-ful night of sleep, he thinks, *I need to call Tricia to see if I can have a session.* His racing thoughts seem not to be settling down. He arrives at work and routinely opens his office. Before his first meeting, he drafts an email to Tricia Thornton: "It's been a while since we met for the parent program when my daughters were in middle school and my son was in high school. I'm wondering if I can come in individually. I remember you mentioned it might be a good idea. Well, I think I'm ready. Do you have any availability in the next week?"

Chapter 8

The Parts of Acknowledgment

After my grandmother's tragic death, fear imprinted a lasting hold within my brain. Loss resurfaced throughout my life and into adulthood, causing my marriage to suffer. My anxious attachment style began to plague me as I craved closeness but at the same time had built a wall of protection around my soul. I relate to C. S. Lewis's idea that "No one ever told me that grief felt so like fear,"[4] because my grief for multiple losses in my life evoked my fear responses to surface all through my life. My idea of God was being covered up by an overwhelming fear that thrust me into a life of falsely needing acceptance, surviving on performance, and being a pleaser.

Dr. Richard Schwartz created a model of therapy called Internal Family Systems (IFS) that states, "We are more like an alliance of different parts, all representing very distinct aspects of what we think of as 'the real me.'"[5] Dr. Schwartz named our core center part as the "self." It is the part that embodies goodness and wholeness. When IFS is blended with Christianity, the self is referred to as the God-image part. I like to refer to this divine center as the True Self. Often we feel that our True Selves may get covered as we go through difficult seasons. However, our True Selves are always the core, staying connected and whole.

In Scripture, there is a nod to this idea that we are made up of parts. In Romans 7:15, Paul talks about his inner struggles: "I don't really understand myself, for I want to do what is right, but I don't do it. Instead, I do what I hate" (NLT). James also laments the inward battle: "What causes fights and quarrels among you? Don't they come from your desires that battle within you?" (James 4:1). Often, it feels there is a battle between our True Selves and other parts. Our True Selves may desire to follow the Christian ways, but our flesh fights to hold on to another view. I see this often in my own life and with my clients. For example, we may know that scrolling on social media is not productive, but we get sucked into the trance of the desire to be "in the know." As Paul infers it is an "inward battle" between our True Selves and our other parts.

The Parts Model

Let's look at Alexander and his parts that rush in to protect his True Self. Did you notice Alexander's rigid routines that he holds on to as life preservers? Because Alexander was a young child when his parents got divorced, he felt he had to be a doer, controller, and thinker. He had to be in charge of his younger brother when his mother had to go back to work. The part of him that, now, is rushing to protect his exiled big feelings is his "doer" part. This is very common; we have seen it with Sally and Lawson too. I know this part well too.

As long as Alexander keeps doing his rigid routines, he will not feel the burdened anxiety and powerlessness as strongly. As a young father, his controlling part tried to rescue him by being a dictator to his children and even his wife. He would put up a wall around himself and try to control all that felt out of control so he could block out his big feelings of self-doubt and worthlessness.

He was bound and determined to be successful as a hedge fund executive. This is when his "thinker" part was strengthened. Alexander's emotional vocabulary was not very developed. He knew a lot of facts and was brilliant in business. As he became more recognized in the financial world, he gained many false affirmations for his perfectionistic tendencies.

Our parts often try to protect us; however, the True Self becomes blurred. Our other parts, like Alexander's doer and thinker parts, rush in to protect us from perceived fears based on past experiences. These other parts are working hard to help us not to feel the threats. Often, our True Selves get covered up by these other protector parts. Unburdening our parts from this protector role is a path to discover our True Selves. We will walk with Alexander as he slowly learns of ways to discover how his big feelings can be a blessing. We will get a glimpse into his journey of discovering his True Self.

The Brain's Role of Acknowledgment

Throughout childhood, the brain goes through three developmental shifts. The limbic region is developed at birth, but the prefrontal cortex does not develop until a person's mid-twenties. The first developmental shift occurs at the age of five to six years old, right as the child enters kindergarten. The second shift occurs at around ten to eleven years old as the child is rounding out of elementary school and moving toward middle school. The last shift is as the child enters high school at age fourteen to fifteen years old. As a child matures and their brain goes through each shift, the prefrontal cortex goes through what I like to refer to as "growth spurts." Has your child ever complained of leg pains during a growth spurt? It is similar in their brains as they grow and their brains prune the neurons that are no longer needed. Your child does not feel actual pain, but we as parents sometimes feel the pain of our children pushing us away and pulling us desperately close, like Velcro.

As the brain shifts, neural pathways are hardwired. Negative neural pathways form if a traumatic experience occurs around one of the growth spurts. Alexander's parents got a divorce right as he was ending fourth grade, at about ten-and-a-half years old. The power of a negative

Brainy Tidbit

Another term for the shifting is called synaptic pruning. It occurs throughout the regions of the brain, but mainly in the prefrontal cortex.

—Beyond Blessed Parenting—

pathway can be so strong it has a lasting impact on adulthood. Often, this is how our attachment styles become more developed. Our parts will gain emotional muscles during the brain's shifts. Do you ever feel that you are fighting your old pathways? Under stress, our brains will go right back to these ingrained circuits, even when they are not healthy. Affirming that our parts are working hard to protect us and getting to know our false selves is a gateway to the power of acknowledgment of our True Selves and God, ultimately opening ourselves to others. When we connect within by acknowledging our difficult feelings, we are able to authentically connect with others.

Spiritual Insights of Acknowledgment

Our beautiful God-formed neuroplastic brains can hold multiple feelings at the same time. We all know moments in our lives when we feel joy and fear or angst and excitement at the same time. At each of the births of my two daughters, I experienced fear of the birthing process and joy for the blessing of my babies. I often tell my child clients it's perfectly normal to feel excitement about starting a new school year while simultaneously feeling anxious about having a new teacher.

Two women in the Bible experienced this juxtaposition of concurrently holding two end-of-the-spectrum feelings. Both were named Mary—one Mary Magdalene, a friend of Jesus, and the other Mary, the mother of Jesus. They went together to the tomb to grieve and to prepare Jesus's body for burial. As they approached the tomb, they were afraid when they found the stone rolled away. Their fear continued when two angels appeared, inquiring why the two Marys had come to the tomb, since their Savior had risen from the dead (Luke 24: 1–10). Their fears were then challenged with unexplainable joy. God made our brains powerfully to be able to hold multiple feelings at the same time. The women were elated with celebration that Jesus had risen from the dead, yet at the same time they felt perplexed at how it happened. Confusion can evoke fear within. Often, we feel multiple feelings at the same time. It is normal, yet it can be tiring.

Feather for Your Day

In Psalm 86:11, David prays to walk in God's truths and to have an undivided heart. When we acknowledge Him in all our ways by noticing and affirming the hard work of our false selves, we open our hearts to wholeness and our True Selves. This can be a newer way of thinking. Affirming all parts of us is freeing our True Selves to shine brightly.

Chapter 9

Using Affirmation to Acknowledge

I noticed that Alexander had a sense of comfort and curiosity as he entered my waiting room. He had sat on the same orange couch with his wife, Julie, just a few years prior. Back then, they had felt tired and overwhelmed, parents of girls who were about eleven and thirteen years old and a son who was about to turn seventeen. At that time, his job had been shifting, and he had felt that Julie and he were at a crossroads in terms of how to parent. One of their girls had been diagnosed with dyslexia and, on top of that, his son's coach (who was also Alexander's business partner) was starting treatment for prostate cancer. Now, he took a deep breath and settled into a feeling of unknown and assurance at the same time.

It's been interesting to watch the movement in my practice from mainly working with children to now also working with their parents as couples and as individuals. Hence, the birth of this book.

Since COVID-19, we all have heard of the increase of statistics of child mental illness. When I read the rising numbers of youth suicide and depression rates, I recognize our culture has a suffering family system. Several years ago, Alexander and Julie had completed my five-session parent program—like marriage therapy but from a parental lens—and had followed up with a few check-ins afterward as well. So now, Alexander caught me up with the latest happenings in his life. After his friend had completed treatment, they started a new company, mainly working as hedge fund managers. We transitioned to what was bringing Alexander in to see me. He shared about the strange reaction he had about his upcoming reunion and how he often felt frustrated, especially about the Nashville traffic. The girls were growing up fast, and he was starting to think about them leaving in three years. He looked at me and said, "Tricia, remember how you taught Julie and me about the two buckets? I feel mine is empty, and frankly, I'm exhausted."

As we make connections with God and within ourselves, we fill our buckets.

Let me take a few minutes to explain the two-bucket concept. Remember the power of the cross-view I shared earlier? We first must attune with God, then ourselves, then our partners, and last with our children. As we make connections with God and within ourselves, we fill our buckets. Only when our buckets are more full are we able to have enough water to fill others' buckets. Two buckets need to be filled each day. The first is that we are seen and heard. The second is that we feel positive power. Once we are seen and heard, then we are empowered to make positive choices. A sandcastle cannot be built with dry sand. I must put some water in a bucket to help mold the structure. Our job as parents is to fill our buckets so we can mold and shepherd our children.

Feather for Your Day

Matthew 22:37–40 states, "Love the Lord your God with all your heart and with all your soul and with all your mind. This is the first and greatest commandment. And the second is like it: 'Love your neighbor as yourself.'

Tools to Use to Learn How to Acknowledge

Alexander vulnerably shared he had been oddly struck by the email about the reunion. After some deciphering, we figured out it was not about seeing his buddies but about the fact that he would have to revisit the pains of losing his dear mentor and coach. After his parents divorced at a pivotal developmental age, he felt lost. He connected with Coach Alan in his freshman advisory group when he got to college. Coach Alan filled his bucket almost daily for the next four years. He even attended Alexander's wedding to say the opening prayer. Alexander had not realized until he was sitting on my therapy office's blue couch in the safety of my space that he felt immensely out of control and floundering after he lost Alan a year and a half ago. His powerlessness showed up through a rise of agitation at anything and everything. Our hearts, souls, and minds will reveal our wounds in one way or another as our bodies can no longer maintain balance. Let's discover how certain tools will help us to acknowledge our feelings and, in time, discover our True Selves.

Connect-with-the-Heart Activity

This method helps to name our feelings, which allows us to acknowledge them so they don't continue to cover up our True Selves. It starts by taking a few deep breaths and gently placing your hand on your heart. Then, name feeling words that come to your mind. I often notice that the first feelings I name are quite strong, such as *unsafe*, *angry*, or *scared*. Then, as I identify these emotions, a shift to more positive feelings like *safe*, *comforted*, and *connected* occurs. By naming our feelings, curiosity is embraced, and we can notice our parts that want to rush in to help us not feel the stored-up negative thoughts.

When parents do this exercise, they are attuning to God and within themselves. Their "seen and heard" buckets receive some drops of water to then feel positive power to help them see and hear their partners, then their children.

Affirming Language

Alexander's second session began with him coming in feeling exasperated with one of his daughters. She had been so demanding and was not listening, and frankly, he felt like she was a fourteen-year-old who was acting like a four-year-old. After reviewing that his daughter was in the middle of a brain shift, it made more sense to him. He was shifting his perspective. He was starting to understand why she was as sassy as a younger child while simultaneously declaring her independence as a teenager.

God does wire the adolescent brain to prepare to flee the nest. Alexander was introduced to the idea of using affirming language during our earlier parent sessions. He needed a gentle reminder. Affirming language is a way for a parent to acknowledge their child's feelings before bringing in redirection. Alexander struggled not to go back to listing all the things his daughter was doing that were bugging him. We paused and did the connect-with-the-heart activity. I empathetically asked him to pause and wonder what part of him was rushing in to try to not feel out of control. After naming the feelings and connecting them with the heart activity, he was able to attune within to receive the empowering tool of affirmation. One of the biggest reasons we shy away from using affirming language is our inner critics or our thinker parts, which try to rescue us from our big feelings. I reminded Alexander of how we learned about affirming language back in our parent program sessions from when his children were younger. We begin to overthink and criticize the need for affirmation. Often, parents feel that by using affirming language, you are giving your child permission to keep doing the negative behaviors. To help make sense of this idea of the importance of using affirming language, let's review an example of a script a parent can use with their child.

You can tailor this to any age and in a variety of scenarios. In this particular scene, the child is a ten-year-old who was just told to put his Nintendo Switch away to get ready for dinner:

PARENT. It's time for dinner in ten minutes. Your game time will be over in five minutes. Be sure to set your timer.

CHILD. Can I have five more minutes, please?!

PARENT. No, I gave you the warning. Five more minutes.

CHILD, *with a raised tone and angry voice.* "You are the worst! You never let me have more time!

PARENT, *after taking three deep breaths and quickly doing the five senses activity.* "Wow! I see and hear that you are feeling angry at me. Hmm, that must be frustrating to feel that way." (*Pauses in silence.*) "I wonder if there is a way for us to figure this out together?"

CHILD: "Yes! Give me more time!"

PARENT: "Yes, that is one way, but we have a rule of twenty minutes of screen time. How about after dinner, we go on a ten-minute walk together just you and me to walk Toby [the dog]?"

CHILD: "Okay." (*Huffs a bit but cracks a smile.*)

This won't always go this seamlessly. However, over time, the parent and child will together feel affirmed. One key fact to note is that by affirming a child's feelings, you are not saying it's okay for the child to be disrespectful. If we redirect first and then try to connect, it sends a message of negativity to the child. Over time, the child will feel shut down and not open to acknowledge his feelings. This unhealthy pattern can lead to a dismissive or avoidant-insecure attachment style. Alexander sighed a bit of relief to take this tool to put into action. We want to connect first by affirming their feelings, then bring in the redirection.

Alexander had an "aha" moment after we reviewed the affirming language script. He realized that he needed to affirm his big feelings within himself first before jumping to his old patterns of performance. He began to feel a weight lift as he realized that all those parenting sessions actually were still paying forward, but this time in his own life as an individual. He began to feel a stronger connection with God and within himself.

Invitation to Acknowledge

Accepting the invitation to acknowledge God first allows affirmation within ourselves and with others. In Luke 9, Jesus predicted His upcoming death for the first time. He declared for us to "take up your cross daily, and follow me" (v. 23). When we choose to acknowledge God in all our ways, we will have more water in our bucket to name our feelings and use affirming language with ourselves and with others. Seeing and hearing God first invites the power of togetherness. Freedom is found in connection. John 8:31–32 declares, "If you hold to my teaching, you are really my disciples. Then you will know the truth, and the truth will set you free."

Feather for Your Day

"Hold" in John 8:31 in Greek is *meno*, which means "to abide, remain, or stay." It is an ongoing state of true and authentic connection.

Journal and Reflection Questions

For Discussion

When have you simultaneously experienced multiple feelings? Name the feelings.

_____

_____

_____

_____

Describe a parenting moment when affirming language would have been helpful.

_____

_____

_____

_____

What fills your "seen and heard" bucket?

_____

_____

_____

_____

A Verse for Acknowledgment

"In all your ways acknowledge Him, and He shall direct your paths."

Proverbs 3:6 NKJV

—Tricia Thornton—

Part 4
Renewal

We change our behavior when the pain of staying the same becomes greater than the pain of changing.

—Dr. Henry Cloud and Dr. John Townsend

Suffer what you have to suffer, but don't suffer what you don't have to suffer.

—Dr. Alison Cook and Kimberly Miller, *Boundaries for Your Soul*

Chapter 10

The Fawning Life of Rose

Rose feels a calmness as she enjoys her hair being colored and styled. The humming of hair dryers brings a sense of peace. A faint tune of calming music is playing that warms her insides.

Ding! A rush of sharp heat permeates Rose's veins. It is like a boulder that just crashed into her serene lakelike moment and splashed her, sending a shock to her nervous system. Her stylist notices a change—Rose's face has drained of color. Rose quietly whispers to her stylist that if she could just finish blowing out her hair . . . She is okay, but she needs to leave. On the way home a flood of memories washes over her like an old breakup song. Too many painful thoughts rush in, but the main one she keeps returning to is herself sitting in that same salon chair and hearing a beep on her phone two years ago. She still remembers "the text" from one of her daughters. It read, *Mom, go to my house now! The children are okay, but there's been a shooting. I'm on my way!* She intellectually knows the text today is not at all like that. It is from her church friend wondering if she is bringing the baskets for the new mothers to the meeting tonight.

However, her emotional brain and heart are having a hard time separating reality from the past. She remembers the details of that day a couple of years ago. Her two youngest grandchildren, who were three and five years old, were with a sitter while their mother, Rose's daughter, was picking up the oldest grandchild (who was eight years old) from school and going to an art class. Her daughter knew Rose was not available to pick up the children that day because of her appointment at the beauty parlor. (She can hear her daughter tease her, *"Mom, it's called a salon."*) The sitter had stopped to get some gas at the village market. This was a loved tradition by her grandchildren along with many other community children. They all felt known and loved by the gas station attendant who had a wonderful memory and often would call the children by name. Community children would go after school or other activities to get treats from the market. As usual that day, the sitter had stopped at the station so the children could get ICEEs as a treat after preschool. Tragically, that day turned out much different from the many other visits. A random robbery occurred in the suburban corner gas station, unfortunately killing the beloved attendant. Many children were present, but no other individuals lost their lives. The children's sitter was the granddaughter of one of Rose's sewing club friends. So, the interweb of relationships went far and wide into the community. Thankfully, the children did not ever see the shooter or the victim being shot, but the sounds of sirens blaring toward the gas station, the screaming of people, and other horrifying images crashed into Rose's grandchildren's young brains. After the memories flood her consciousness, she battles within herself to turn off the fearful thoughts. She tells herself, *Get yourself together, Rose! You have taken care of everyone for two years. So, just concentrate on finishing the welcome baskets for church. You have to leave to pick up the grandchildren from soccer practice and get them home before Sarah gets home from work.*

She goes over to the cupboard to pull out the list of items that must be included in the gift sets. Out falls a flyer she has not seen for a couple of years: "Recovery Group for Grandparents," it reads. She feels a nudge. Another inner dialogue starts as she recalls more memories. *Oh, that dear Tricia was so understanding during those groups. Hmm, I wonder if she is still seeing any children from that awful day?* Memories of sitting on what some moms had deemed "the couch of comfort" in Tricia Thornton Therapy's waiting room as she waited for the grandchildren to finish their play therapy appointments fill her mind. The morning after that horrible Wednesday, the three children saw a therapist, Mrs. Tricia. They worked with her for a few months. Rose remembers Tricia extending an invitation for her to come in because she was holding a lot together for the whole family. She comes back to the present moment and smiles as if the Holy Spirit nudges her to pick up the phone. She winks to herself and puts a reminder sticky note on her Bible: "Call Tricia." Off she goes to the soccer field with snacks in tow and the five new-mother baskets in the back of her van.

—Tricia Thornton—   99

Chapter 11

The Continuum of Renewal

For the longest time, I did not think of myself as having experienced trauma. I always thought severe abuse or living in a war zone was what psychology referred to as trauma. As I started my therapeutic journey back in graduate school at Denver Seminary, I first heard about trauma as being on a continuum. In 1995, I wrote a paper in my counseling graduate program that put together a timeline of my life events from birth to the present day, which ended at that time with my parents' divorce. A few significant life events included a horrible car crash, my maternal grandmother's sudden death in the driveway of my childhood home, and a home invasion three weeks later. These are the ones that occurred just in my first six years. I experienced multiple losses throughout my childhood and teen years. I have endured major medical events including a heart procedure for SVT and two removed ovarian tumors.

My husband and I had many roadblocks rise up in our marriage. While I was near finishing *Blessing From Fear*, my Nashville community suffered a tragic school shooting at The Covenant School. I continue to work with families from that traumatic event. You can read much more about my journey and the effects of fear on my brain in my first book. I often say writing *Blessing From Fear* not only saved my marriage but healed my True Self as well.

Trauma is defined as an experience that evokes a significant emotional response. A trauma continuum goes from the loss of a pet or job to surviving a school shooting to living in a war zone. Trauma is trauma, as far as the brain is concerned. There is also a timeline for the aftermath of a trauma, from pre-disaster to a honeymoon, which is a strange high that occurs shortly after the experience, to disillusionment as shock wears off and reality sets in. The line continues toward renewal with a reconstruction phase as new beginnings occur. All along are triggers and setbacks that cause an individual to bob along like floating on a raft in the middle of the ocean during a thunderstorm.

The Brain's Role in Renewal

One of the most common responses children experience after a trauma is an increase in meltdowns. If a child was sensitive or anxious before a traumatic event, then after, the behaviors are exaggerated. Rose, her grandchildren, and, adult daughter all had more tantrums after the gas station shooting. It is helpful to understand the why and how of tantrums. When a child (or an adult) feels a big feeling, the message in the brain gets lodged in the emotional center (limbic region), and an "almond tantrum" occurs. I like to call this kind of meltdown an almond tantrum because it is when the message received from the five senses gets stuck in the almond-shaped amygdala, causing a hijacked effect. Dr. Daniel Siegel refers to this as "flipping our lid."[6] The mammal brain's responses are ignited when the "almond" (or amygdala) is flipped. This is when the fear responses take over. It is as if the almond is then driving the car doing donuts in the middle of a busy highway at rush hour. The prefrontal cortex region, or the executive center, is then holding on for dear life in the passenger seat.

If a child was sensitive or anxious before a traumatic event, then after, the behaviors are exaggerated.

The child must sense a safe connection to slow down the swerving car and put the prefrontal cortex back in the driver's seat. As we have discussed, we know now if a child is to experience an authentic connection, the adult caregiver must first connect with God, then within themselves. The prefrontal cortex is like the upstairs of a house. Connection is the staircase bridging to the downstairs limbic region. As with the timeline of trauma, renewal can occur over time as positive energy connections transfer from an adult to a child.

—Tricia Thornton—

Spiritual Insights of Renewal

Jesus certainly did not go through life without trials and tribulations. One of the most manlike experiences we get the blessing to glean from is when Jesus went with His disciples to get away and pray before He was brutally crucified. The realness of His expressed agony gives us hope. He left the disciples to go be by Himself to cry out, "Father, if you are willing, please take this cup of suffering away from me. Yet I want your will to be done, not mine" (Luke 22:42 NLT). This sacrificial prayer was a pleading cry out to His Father. Jesus knew He was about to be emotionally and physically tortured. His brain did feel all the big feelings; however, in His perfection, Jesus was in a completely renewed and connected state of His True Self, creating a holy submission response.

On this side of heaven, we are not able to truly submit to the Lord. We can, however, strive toward a renewal of spirit, soul, and body as 1 Thessalonians 5:23 acclaims: "May God himself, the God of peace, sanctify you through and through. May your whole spirit, soul and body be kept blameless at the coming of our Lord Jesus Christ."

Feather for Your Day

The charge from Paul rings loudly as a sweet whisper to our souls: "So we do not lose heart. Though our outer self is wasting away, our inner self is being renewed day by day."
2 Corinthians 4:16 ESV

Chapter 12

The Responses to Renewal

Rose enters the peaceful therapy room. She immediately feels that same hot sensation she felt last week at the salon. It's an unfamiliar yet all too familiar feeling that has begun to surface more often. She notices a decorative cross resting on the table next to me and feels a bit more at ease. She remembers sitting in a therapist's office years ago as a mother of three teenagers. Back then, it made sense why she was so tired. She was a teacher and raising children with a husband who traveled often for work. Now she is retired and enjoys many hobbies but seems to have less time for herself and her dear husband of forty-seven years.

She quickly gets out of her head and asks me how I am doing. She asks about my family and how the sales of my first book are going. She loves to hear how others are doing. I notice that if I don't gently shift the conversation, Rose will keep genuinely inquiring about me. In therapy, I welcome questions about my life, but I also am aware it can indicate someone may feel nervous or may be stuck in a fawn response mode.

A Common Response to Renewal

Sally, Rose, and I all tend to feel a common response when our brains sense something that is not right. Fear can be real or perceived. The response is the same whether it is an actual fear-producing event or an inner-sensed situation. I softly redirected Rose to tell me a bit about what was bringing her in for therapy. After hearing how exhausted she was feeling, I shared with her a few more tips about the common fawn response. It is often difficult to detect a fawn response because it can look like being a helper and being nice. One of the most telling signs that someone is fawning is feeling overly tired and irritable. This reaction may be rooted in growing up in a family where you don't want to shake the apple cart too much. Maybe the individual had a parent who yelled often or a sibling who needed a lot of attention. It can surface as a feeling of having to walk on eggshells, and being nice and helpful can become a way of survival or protection from feeling overwhelmed.

Brainy Tidbit

One of the four fear responses will come online in the limbic region when the senses recognize a scared sense of feeling out of control.

Boundaries Are the Key

Most people who fawn struggle with having healthy boundaries. Sometimes putting up a boundary can feel rude or selfish. But before we go too far, let's define *boundaries*. Think of a border or property line. Those are what we call *physical boundaries*. Emotional boundaries can be defined as the lines where one person ends and another begins. If you experience any of the following four questions or thoughts regularly, that may indicate blurred boundaries:

- Why does this person always expect me to drop everything and cater to their needs?
- I don't have time to do all this!
- I am so tired, and frankly, I don't care anymore!
- Why do I often become triggered by my child's big emotions?

If you walk away with one key concept to remember about boundaries, let it be this: If you find yourself tired and feeling irritable because you feel someone is demanding too much from you, pause and look inward. Recall the discussion about parents connecting within themselves first so they can connect with their children to affirm and empower a healthy response. It's the same with having healthy emotional boundaries within themselves before expecting their children to have healthy boundaries. Modeling is the key that opens the door to a renewed spirit.

—Tricia Thornton—

Feather for Your Day

Deuteronomy 30:19 states, "Today, I have given you the choice between life and death, between blessings and curses" (NLT). Intentionally developing healthy emotional boundaries is like opening a window to receive a breeze of blessings.

Tools to Use to Respond to Renewal

Rose came back for several sessions. We continued to explore when she felt her fear responses come online. We also revisited the idea of boundaries and how to feel comfortable putting them in place within herself and with her daughter. Because of her anxious attachment style, she tended to put up walls around herself for protection. She realized she had allowed the busyness of helping others to shield her from facing the fears of the unknown. Even thoughts about her own death were seeming to surface more lately.

Our focus in therapy shifted to ways she could encourage her grandchildren and her daughters. The hardest part was not to overstep by telling her daughter how to parent or undermining her daughter's parenting. That was a delicate road, so we often did the "connect-with-the-heart" activity during our sessions to check in. One healthy response was for Rose to learn how to have more flexibility. Often it is difficult to honor ourselves while staying connected with others. When we lose our individualism, integration cannot occur. Think of integration as harmony or balance. There are two individuals; each has their own feelings. Then, there is the relationship. If each individual is connected within and has healthy boundaries, the relationship then can have an integrated balance. Two ways we can be linked to another and still honor ourselves is through rubber band thinking and Hula-Hoop boundaries.

Rubber Band Thinking

Imagine a river and there are banks on either side. The river represents your mind. On one riverbank, there are lots of sticks and rocks, causing swirls and even some rapids. This side of the river represents when we are drawn to drama and chaos in our lives. Along the other shore are orderly rows of neatly lined trees. The bank represents when we have a fixed mindset and are not flexible. Ultimately, we want our boats (or our thoughts) to float down the middle of a calm river. The river represents having a balanced, harmonious state of being. However, our boats are often pulled to one side or the other. Neither side is necessarily better or worse than the other. We all need order, and we all need to embrace a bit of chaos. The key to balancing the boat and returning to a calmer middle is to have what I like to call "rubber band thinking."

In explaining this to children, I will get out a rubber band and ask what makes it able to be stretched. Flexibility is needed. I also have a box of items, some are not bendable, like a rock or a screw, and some items are, like a pipe cleaner or a piece of ribbon. The child will reach into the box and name if the items are flexible or rigid. Rubber band thinking occurs when we are able to balance. We will embrace the chaos and not allow the loops of fearful thoughts to take over. As well, we will not be pulled into believing all has to be perfect. We are able to be flexible and adapt to shifting situations that arise. This is certainly not easy to do for adults or children, so it is a skill that will keep improving over time.

Children learn from visual everyday life experiences. To strengthen rubber band thinking, when you're out and about, talk about things like how you wish you could speed up to get to the practice on time, but we have to obey traffic laws. Parents can also model the flexibility of rubber band thinking by recalling a time in their lives when plans changed and their "river" changed. Children often enjoy hearing about how a parent used a tool in their own life. Parenting is not about perfection but about connection.

Parenting is not about perfection but about connection.

Hula-Hoop Boundaries

One day, Rose came in for her session particularly exasperated. Her ten-year-old granddaughter was struggling with some girl drama at school. She had been having more tantrums lately like ones of a toddler. Rose was looking for a way to explain the concept of emotional boundaries. I smiled and asked if Rose could Hula-Hoop. She giggled and said, "Why yes! I'm quite good as a matter of fact!" I then inquired if she was born a good Hula-Hooper. She told some fun stories about having contests with her brothers as children. She remembered often practicing in her room because she was bound and determined to win the game of who could keep up the hoop the longest.

I pointed out that most people have to learn to keep the Hula-Hoop spinning and not fall to the floor. It's up to us if we lower our hoop or not. It's the same way with emotional boundaries. In my play therapy room with my child clients (and even in my office with my adult clients), I will get two stuffed animals and put one in the middle of a Hula-Hoop. I tell the child to imagine the other stuffy has a hoop around it too. I explain that we are all responsible for keeping our hoops up.

It's a great way to tie in physical boundaries as well. I do say that, sadly, sometimes a hoop is not respected, and someone touches us when we tell them not to, but hopefully, most people respect our physical boundaries. If a friend (another stuffy) says some unkind words to us and we have our hoop spinning, the words cannot get through our safe space. It's like we have a shield of armor around us. Teaching children about emotional boundaries is a gift. A child's brain craves boundaries to promote their rubber band thinking skills to strengthen. Rose was reminded that as she continues to strengthen her flexibility and her emotional boundaries, she will feel renewed to connect with others. Rose was so excited about teaching these concepts to her grandchildren that she ordered two Hula-Hoops from Amazon before leaving the session!

The Calming Gift of Renewal

The journey to not conforming but being "transformed by the renewing of your mind" (Romans 12:2) can be long and winding.

Rose's grandchildren had experienced a traumatic event and had many sleepless nights in their parents' bed, but they were slowly embracing the truth that God's love will calm your fears. I have carried a loss all my life, and I keep trusting that God covers me with His wings as promised in Psalm 91:4. I hold fast to this truth to renew my mind, spirit, and body and to "Guard your heart above all else, for it determines the course of your life" (Proverbs 4:23 NLT).

Journal and Reflection Questions

For Discussion

When have you experienced a traumatic event? How does it influence your parenting?

_____

_____

_____

_____

When have you cried out to God to take away pain (emotional, spiritual, or physical)?

_____

_____

_____

_____

In what areas of your life do you feel that you allow your Hula-Hoop boundaries to drop?

_____

_____

_____

_____

A Verse for Renewal

"Do not conform to the pattern of this world, but be transformed by the renewing of your mind. Then you will be able to test and approve what God's will is—his good, pleasing and perfect will."

Romans 12:2

—Tricia Thornton—   115

Part 5
Forgiveness

Once your discomfort gets greater than your fear of change, you'll live differently.

—Preacher Mike, First Baptist Church of Indian Trail

Forgiveness is not an occasional act; it is a permanent attitude.

—Martin Luther King Jr., *Strength to Love*

Chapter 13

The Spinning Life of Francine

The last time Francine went to see a therapist was a challenging session. She and her husband had to tell their two young daughters that they were going to get a divorce. The girls are now fourteen and sixteen years old. Their school counselor has suggested Francine seek out some parental therapy because her fourteen-year-old is struggling in school with depression and anxiety. The school counselor felt that what she could provide was limited by her other counseling duties, so seeking an outside professional would be helpful. Francine remembers attending a parent seminar at the girls' elementary school and enjoying the therapist speaker. She gives her a call and is able to make an appointment with her the following week.

Francine comes in hot to the first session, for she is still reeling from the day before. An angry energy surrounds her, and I can tell she is wound up and full of anxiety. She sits down and lets out a huff. She knocks over her water bottle and says a cuss word. She looks at me like a child who is about to get in trouble, and I remind her it is okay to say whatever she would like in this safe space. I suggest she feel free to share with me what rattled her. She proceeds to share the details:

> I woke up and was in a bit of a hurry. My brain was foggy because I had my Friendsgiving the night before. The girls complained all morning that I had no time to make their favorite breakfast. They just don't get it! They left, and I rushed around trying to straighten up, and then, of course, she called right then! My ex's wife called to ask if we could change up the calendar. They were trying to take all the girls—oh, they have two of their own, plus mine. Ha! That is a lot of weddings!—anyway, she wanted to see if the girls could be with them for spring break because they wanted to take them on a Disney cruise. My girls seem a bit old for it, but my ex's four- and six-year-old girls would love it. As I was running around trying to finish my morning checklist, I tripped over my daughter's iPad and about broke it. I wanted to kick it across the room and screamed a few cuss words out to the universe!
>
> So that happened. Then I rushed to put the laundry basket in my youngest daughter's room. I must have been going so fast that a note blew off her dresser. I

glanced at it and noticed it was to her best friend and was about how much she was struggling daily with sad thoughts. I started to feel a rush of angst come over me. I reminded myself that she has a therapist and is getting the needed help. Then, as I was trying to get out of the house, my sister called to ask when the girls and I were coming down for Christmas. Ugh, I didn't even tell you that my mother just got diagnosed with early Alzheimer's. So, that was my day!

Chapter 14

The Reality of Forgiveness

The road toward Home is a long and arduous one. As a Christian believer, I am called to keep my sights on God, even amid pain. This is certainly not easy to do. Our protector parts want to rush in constantly, and we battle to uncover our sacred God-image core. When I sat at the beach cottage to outline and begin writing this book, I wrestled with God about what to call this principle. I wanted to call it "letting go," but I felt a genuine nudge to call it "forgiveness." I wrote it and then would erase it—yes, I actually write my books with pencil and paper—and then write again. I would take a bike ride and come back to the inner tugging. Finally, I realized I didn't want to call it forgiveness because it is a touchy subject and, personally, a raw one. I struggled with how to be gentle yet bold at the same time. I know my brain can hold multiple feelings simultaneously, so I am trusting God that these words will safely yet powerfully be received.

—Tricia Thornton—

The Tree of Forgiveness

The reality of forgiveness is it has to do with loss, acceptance, and freedom. Let's touch on each of these points. There are whole books on this subject, so I will not be able to do a deep dive, but I will touch on what I like to call the "tree of forgiveness." A strong-rooted tree will grow tall for years. A holy tree lives forever. The roots are the Trinity, made of the strength and tenderness of the omnipotent Father, Son, and Holy Spirit. From the roots grows an all-powerful trunk that will not bend. It is the cross on which Jesus was crucified. From the sacrificial loss Jesus felt, the mighty branches grow forth. One main branch is acceptance, and the other central branch is freedom. Because of the Trinity roots and the cross trunk, we can receive and accept the invitation to follow God. The invitation does not depend on us but on the cross. From this gift comes a divine freedom that will keep giving birth to new branches. Forgiveness is like the leaves that never fall off.

A holy tree lives forever.

The Brain's Role in Forgiveness

Are you familiar with quantum physics? I promise to make this easy to understand. One of the most fascinating phenomena of quantum physics is the QZE (Quantum Zeno Effect). "It stipulates that your brain becomes what you focus on and how you focus."[7] That means the more energy spent on specific thoughts, the stronger the brain's neural pathways to form those thoughts. In my own life "fearful thoughts dictated my actions. Even in my marriage, fear was winning the battles way too often."[8] Francine was allowing fear to become her focus. I tend to have the fawn response as my most common response; however, fight will arise from time to time. Francine's anger fight response was a loop that entrapped her often. She often found herself blaming others and trying to control all with her tone of voice and strong words. I like to visualize a hamster on a wheel going around and around. It's interesting that they tend to be more active at night, because so do our negative thoughts. The more we dwell on them, running on that wheel, the more negative emotions will be present in our lives.

Clients often ask me, "Why do I keep doing the unhealthy action or replaying the negative event when I know it is not helpful?" Remember, neural pathways form according to what we focus on most. Think of your brain as a computer system. The adverse thoughts are a file that doesn't have a place to be categorized. It's like the file is just floating around on your computer. We have to choose to focus on the strong, holy roots of the Trinity to help our thoughts become more life-giving. Our minds will then be able to do as Deuteronomy 30:19 says and "choose life." Then, the brain's computer system will have a healthy place to house the file.

> **Brainy Tidbit**
>
> A child's prefrontal cortex is not fully developed. So it is easier for meltdowns to be the way they process negative thoughts.

The Spiritual Role of Forgiveness

In her recap video of Titus 1–3, Tara-Leigh Cobble encourages us by saying, "Grace is a change agent."[9] Grace is the gift that God gives us all through Christ's death on the cross, even though we don't deserve it. Grace allows us to receive God's forgiveness and then forgive others. We can embrace forgiveness and begin to let go, but that does not at all mean we will forget the pain of another's actions. It often can feel like a wrestling match. Jacob, in Genesis 32:22–32, wrestles with an angel all night. He is desperately trying to make sense of his life. He finally gets to a place of surrender and acceptance that allows the freedom of forgiveness to bless him. The most complex and foundational part of your faith journey is the moment you receive forgiveness.

Feather for Your Day

Psalm 36:7 answers, "How precious is your unfailing love, O God! All humanity finds shelter in the shadow of your wings" (NLT). We have the choice to live in the shadows of fear or in the shadows of His wings.

Chapter 15

Freedom Leads to Forgiveness

In another session, Francine entered my therapy room discouraged. Her fight response was still present but looked a bit different from the previous angry tone. She stated with a downcast expression, "I'm tired. I just don't feel anyone appreciates all I do. I know my girls are egocentric teenagers, but seriously, why can't they at least acknowledge all I do for them!" She recalled her mother working so hard to care for her and her sister after their father left when she was five. Many nights, her mom was so tired she was unable to help with Francine's school projects or homework. Over the years, Francine's loss and anger over the abandonment she felt seemed to have taken over her thoughts. In other sessions, Francine and I had done a lot of work about the early sexual abuse she received from a neighborhood boy when she was in her elementary years. We had discussed how her anger about the abuse was often triggered by present life events. This was a complex trauma layer that was painful to work through. I gently reminded her of the quantum physics phenomenon of QZE. I asked Francine when was the last time she felt her own love language was given to her? More importantly, when did she give herself the attention and affirmation she desperately craved?

We must first attune with God, then ourselves, next with a partner, and then our children.

Gary Chapman first coined the idea of the 5 Love Languages.[10] When parents come for the first session of my parent coaching program, I have them complete an inventory to determine their love language. This is linked to the cross of connection. We must first attune with God, then ourselves, next with a partner, and then our children. In the case of a single parent like Francine, the "partner" connection can happen with a trusted friend. The connection will involve the 5 Love Languages, which are:

1. *Quality Time*: This refers to receiving focused attention. It is about quality versus quantity.

2. *Physical Touch*: This one means that when someone receives touch from another, they feel loved. This can be small touches of a hug, a high five, a pat on the back, or a snuggle on the couch.

3. *Acts of Service*: This language refers to when something is done for someone, such as someone else

helping to pick up dirty clothes, helping to finish a project, arranging a date night from start to finish (including getting a sitter!), and taking out the trash.

4. *Receiving Gifts*: This one refers to when someone appreciates receiving a gift. The gift's monetary value is usually not as important as the care and time put into the gift idea and the effort to make or purchase the gift.

5. *Words of Affirmation*: This language refers to when someone feels love from words of encouragement. A verbal statement, written note, or even an emoji can be Words of Affirmation.[11]

We can often determine our love language by noticing what we give to others. We tend to give what we'd like to receive. My love language is Words of Affirmation. My husband's is Quality Time. If my husband gives me flowers, I really appreciate it, but if he writes a note with the bouquet, I light up. We have determined that going out to dinner or taking walks when I am not as distracted are ways for him to feel his love language. One of my daughter's is Quality Time, and the other's is Physical Touch. My oldest will feel loved when I sit with her to look at reels that mean a lot to her. My youngest often puts her arms out for hugs, even at eighteen. Trust me, I don't always have the time or even want to sit and watch reels with my oldest, but I try to fill her bucket with intention, even if I am bone-tired. (By the way, if it is late at night, I will say, "How about we watch five, and then we can look at more tomorrow when I am a bit more rested?" This is a boundary!)

—Tricia Thornton—

Tools to Use to Embrace Forgiveness

Francine's father leaving her at five years old instilled negative messages into her brain. The sexual abuse also plagued Francine as she began to explore being in a romantic relationship. She grew up feeling she was not worthy of someone else's love. She seemed to attract unhealthy people into her life, especially regarding romantic relationships. Over several months, Francine and I embraced the idea that, because of epigenetics, we have the power to change our neuroplastic brains. In the empowering book *Finding Meaning*, David Kessler asserts, "The mind can be cruel in grief."[12] Slowly, Francine began to see that when her teenage girls were not acknowledging her efforts, she felt the shadows of fear from when she felt abandoned by her father as a little girl creep in. She started to be able to rewrite the negative stories by cherishing forgiveness from God and ultimately beginning not to be controlled by anger and bitterness. In therapy, Francine learned how to use the 5 Love Languages and signals to help her to embrace forgiveness.

Giving Love Languages to Yourself

We can all surmise how intentionally giving love languages can positively affect relationships. With the cross of connection in mind, we also need to give love languages to ourselves. So, be cognizant of ways to give to yourself so you can then fill another's bucket. Then, with some water in your bucket as a parent, you can notice another's cues that they need their love language to be intentionally given. Parents may use positive self-talk statements to give Words of Affirmation to themselves. A fifteen-minute walk can be quality time away from technology. A red light therapy session can serve as a gift to yourself. A yoga routine that stretches the body is a form of physical touch. Unloading the dishwasher to fun music can make an act of service feel more self-loving.

Using Signals

Many times, I will guide parents and children of all ages to come up with a verbal or nonverbal cue they can give one another to communicate that they need their love language at that moment. Children are visual, so signals can serve as beautiful ways to authentically walk up the connection staircase. Francine and I decided that she and her adolescent daughters would benefit from using signals with one another to help rewrite the negative messages that came flooding into Francine's mind. This requires vulnerability because you're stating your needs. A younger child may look at their mom and pat her own head, which signals, "I need a hug" or "I need you to put your phone down and hear about my day." Another signal may be a thumbs-down that says, "I need some alone time, and then I'd like to hear an affirming statement." In sessions, we will review signals and make a chart of their meanings. Parents can also give signals to their children. Francine learned to move her head side to side to tell her girls she needed a "Thank you for folding the laundry."

Children are visual, so signals can serve as beautiful ways to authentically walk up the connection staircase.

The Freedom of Forgiveness

The road to embracing forgiveness is not always easy. Feelings of insecurity and unworthiness can tempt our minds. The fact is we don't deserve God's forgiveness, but because of His grace we are given the gift to embrace the freedom of forgiveness. When we feel fully seen versus not seen, or "empty-seen," we experience an emotional safety that allows us to trust the gift of grace. Being fully seen includes being loved, cherished, valued, and known. Being empty-seen can bring on loneliness, being misunderstood, and feeling unnoticed and unknown. When we are truly present with another, we are positioned to be fully seen. Francine continued to fully see God, herself, and others. Slowly, she began to embrace that she was loved and fully seen by her heavenly Father. Throughout Psalm 139 we are comforted to know that God fully sees us:

> For you created my inmost being;
>> you knit me together in my mother's womb.
> I praise you because I am fearfully and wonderfully made;
>> your works are wonderful,
>> I know that full well.
> My frame was not hidden from you
>> when I was made in the secret place,
>> when I was woven together in the depths of the earth.
> Your eyes saw my unformed body;
>> all the days ordained for me were written in your book
>> before one of them came to be. (vv. 13–16)

When we are truly present with another, we are positioned to be fully seen.

—Tricia Thornton—

Journal and Reflection Questions

For Discussion

What do you tend to focus on most in your life? What dominates
your energy?

_____

_____

_____

_____

Have you ever felt like you have wrestled with God?

_____

_____

_____

_____

What is your primary love language? What about the love languages of your children?

_____

_____

_____

_____

A Verse for Forgiveness

"Brothers and sisters, I do not consider myself yet to have taken hold of it. But one thing I do: Forgetting what is behind and straining toward what is ahead."

Philippians 3:13

Part 6
Balance

Balance is not something you find, it's something you create.

—Jana Kingsford, *UNJUGGLED*

Happiness is not a matter of intensity but of balance and order and rhythm and harmony.

—Thomas Merton, *No Man Is an Island*

Chapter 16

The Distracted Life of Brooke

"Mama, Mama, wake up!" Springing out of bed in a daze, Brooke sees her redheaded three-year-old waiting for her to go into action and do all the "mom things." She suddenly remembers her nightmare, in which she was running down a hallway and could not find the right door to open to get to her children's rooms. She tries to shake it off but is jolted by the realness of the dream. She thinks, *Okay, get with it! Everyone is waiting for you!*

A glimpse of relief comes over her when she discovers her oldest did not wet the bed. She mutters, "At least that is one thing I don't have to do today: Change her sheets!" She goes into the nursery to wake her dear one-and-a-half-year-old, who has a fabulous bed head of brown curls like his daddy. She quickly gets both children to look somewhat cute. Check that off the unending list of duties—until you-know-what hits the fan!

Her precious but sassy "threenager" screams, "I don't want to wear this! It itches!" Brooke runs into the kitchen to find her redhead completely naked. "Ugh, okay, here we go!" Her husband tries to help but gets distracted by the unfinished cabinet he started to repair last weekend. She reminds him that their son's follow-up doctor's appointment is today at 10:00 a.m. She pleads, "Please don't be late." Her daughter finally settles down and agrees to a purple dress with no tights. *Well, she'll freeze, but who really cares at this point? Her teacher will give me that "Bless her heart" smile again.*

Out the door, to the car, and finally to preschool and Parent's Day Out. She can hear her mama and daddy saying in her head, *"Therefore, do not worry about tomorrow, for tomorrow will worry about itself. Each day has enough trouble of its own."*[14] She rolls her eyes and mutters, "Yes, it damn straight does have enough trouble!"

Chapter 17

The Juxtaposition of Balance

Running, running, running—that is how I feel most of my life has gone. I remember the surprised reactions I received when I told a few people I was writing my first book. People who knew me were taken aback that I could slow down enough to write. Sometimes, we don't have a choice but to slow down the treadmill so we don't get thrown off like the funny reels of people getting propelled backward. Several medical issues in my past forced me to slow down for a little while and try to balance the internal pressure I had absorbed. My hypervigilant ADHD brain was wired to be "on go" most of the time. Nothing quite got my attention until my husband and I were forced into what appeared to be roadblocks in our marriage. Simultaneously, our two daughters were facing several medical issues. When I finally realized that my running speed would only add to the turmoil, I began to grasp the necessity of balance. By no means have I fully embraced a more balanced eternal and external state; however, I have made several shifts. As I wrote *Blessing From Fear*, the juxtaposition of balance really began to make sense. I realized throughout my life, I had been racing away from the robbers rather than toward the holy prize.

> **I realized throughout my life, I had been racing away from the robbers rather than toward the holy prize**

The Influence of False Selves

While I was in graduate school at Denver Seminary, one of my professors challenged our class to discover and name our false selves. That powerful assignment ignited a passion that eventually birthed my love for therapy and writing. A false self is a persona that one develops as a way to protect one's True Self. That same professor recommended I read a book by Sue Monk Kidd called *When the Heart Waits*. I was searching for meaning, purpose, and direction from losses and changes in my life, including my parents' divorce when I was twenty-three. There are many false selves, but two that Kidd describes in her book began to sink in.[15] Each of these false selves will still surface today, but now I have more tools in my toolbox so I begin to feel more balanced.

Good Little Girl with the Curl

This false self started to emerge at a young age for me. After the tragic loss of my grandmother and the robbery, I began to receive and believe the message that what we show the outside world is of utmost importance. Growing up in the South also solidified a potent message: "Be pleasing, demure, compliant, conforming, docile, and sweet. Obtain what you need or want through charm, not directness. Be poised on the outside regardless of the chaos on the inside. Above all, smile."[16] My "little Tricia" inner child still feels the sting of that statement even in my mid-fifties. The contrast between the need for balance and inner connectedness has always fought the intense fight of my fear responses.

Chicken Little

This false self may have had roots in my younger years, but the fruit of it did not bloom until I was older. It is coined from the childhood lore about Henny Penny, the chicken who worried and fretted that the sky was falling. During my early years of motherhood, this false self grew in strength. Those worries then began to shift my brain. According to the QZE, I would stay stuck in situations that caused me to be anxious rather than evolve to find a balanced state. My smiling mask covered the worry that I felt on the inside. Maybe I didn't scream "The sky is falling!" but I did feel worried about almost every area of my life.

The Brain's Role in Balance

The vagus nerve is one of the most essential pieces of the brain's structure that affects our ability to be present within and achieve the cross of connection, which will lead to balance. The "tenth cranial nerve" runs from the brain to the gut. As the longest nerve in our bodies, it is quite crucial to basic functions such as breathing and digestion. The vagus nerve is part of the parasympathetic nervous system and is needed to calm the sympathetic nervous system during times of stress and anxiety. There are several ways to activate the vagus nerve. Whether through breathwork, drinking bitters like dandelion root tea, tapping, humming, whistling, using red light therapy, or laughter, our bodies need to activate this critical cranial nerve in order to be balanced.

> ## *Brainy Tidbit*
>
> The physical and emotional roles of balance are intertwined. In more recent years, in neuroscience, it has been discovered that the strength of the brain's cerebellum, which controls movement and balance, is linked to the strength of the prefrontal cortex. Standing on one leg can affect our physical balance as well as our emotional regulating balance.

The Spiritual Role of Balance

Often, I feel like Brooke when she rolled her eyes at the verse about not being worried about tomorrow. When life around you feels

—Beyond Blessed Parenting—

like it is falling apart, it is hard to feel balanced, and often it feels we become disconnected from God and from ourselves. My anxious part wants to keep me in an agitated state because it thinks it's helping me not to feel fear. Remember, our brains will regurgitate old patterns, even if they are unhealthy, because they are familiar. As we journey through the aftermath of a traumatic experience, sometimes negative emotions feel safer and more comfortable. In Psalm 23, David encourages us, "Even though I walk through the darkest valley, I will fear no evil, for you are with me; your rod and your staff, they comfort me" (v. 4). Brooke and I both may react to fear in different ways, but we both don't wish to feel angst. The word *through* is a key preposition in the verse. David did not say we should run *around* or jump *over* the valley but go *through* it. The more we love, the more we will feel grief, because loss and love cannot be disconnected. The more parents love their children, the more they will hurt when their children hurt. Authentic connection is strengthened when we balance within ourselves.

Feather for Your Day

The Lord implored the Israelites worry: "The Lord will fight for you; you need only to be still" (Exodus 14:14). Will we choose to allow the "pillar of cloud" to protect us, or will we choose to let the confusion and imbalance be our shadow?

—Tricia Thornton—

Chapter 18

The Three P's of Balance

Brooke and Mark came in for their third of my five-session parent program. They were relieved to immediately share the good news from their son's follow-up cardiology appointment. The results showed that he did not have a heart defect, but they wanted to keep an eye on him over the next year. I could see a cautious look of relief in Brooke's eyes. We sat for a bit and allowed each of us to feel the positive energy before reviewing everything we had touched on in our previous sessions: their love languages, their attachment styles, emotional Hula-Hoop boundaries, rubber band thinking, co-regulation, and using affirming languages. Today's subject was all about the three P's of balance. I noticed Mark got out his phone. Brooke shot him a look, but he reassured her he wanted to take notes. We all giggled, for we had worked on how Mark's ADHD brain functioned and how Brooke's ambivalent-insecure attachment style was triggered when she felt Mark's lack of focus.

The Brain's Smoke Detector

Before we dove in, they told me about the morning their three-year-old had a royal meltdown over her itchy clothes. Brooke described the almond tantrum, and I noticed Mark was getting distracted by the leaf blower outside the window. Brooke exasperatedly huffed, "Seriously, it's like I have a third child!" I redirected them and explained why their redheaded cutie-pie was flipping her lid over her clothes. It is hard to remember that there is a message behind every behavior. To reengage Mark, I asked him, "What happens when Brooke is toasting a bagel and a little piece of bread gets stuck in the bottom of the toaster?" We all agreed smoke would rise, and the awfully loud smoke detector would start blaring. I explained that their daughter, through her sense of touch, felt the scratching shirt. A message was sent to the thalamus through the senses. The message then got stuck in the limbic region. The amygdala is like the smoke detector in our house. Its only job is to alert that there is danger. It does not know if the whole house is burning down or if it's just a piece of the bagel at the bottom of the toaster.

It is hard to remember that there is a message behind every behavior.

Their daughter's brain sensed fear as if the house was burning down, but it was just an itchy shirt. She may have remembered the last time she wore that shirt; she felt trapped in it all day and could not feel "safe." We all agreed that the shirt was not the real issue, but it was that she did not want to be away from her mommy and daddy. Often, children with some separation anxiety will react to a sensory overload. It was like her brain tricked her. Maybe the shirt did really itch, but the bigger deal was that she felt alone and powerless.

Brainy Tidbit

The brain cues for safety twenty-four seven. It's like a military radar screen alerting when danger is coming. The staircase of connection will cue safety between one brain and another brain. Between the upstairs brain (the prefrontal cortex) and the downstairs brain (the limbic region) an invisible staircase links the two floors. That staircase is the power of the cross of connection. Connecting is the key that helps to strengthen the balance of the two regions of the brain.

We reviewed the affirming language tool they could use to redirect her when there was another itchy-shirt scenario. Knowing the why may not change the event, but it may give us the power to choose to be intentional in seeking balance.

—Tricia Thornton—

Tools to Use to Embrace Balance

Talking about the smoke detector in our brains was a perfect segway into discussing the three P's. I asked Brooke if she ever felt like she was in the middle of the circus as a juggler trying to keep all the balls in the air. She laughed and said, "Yes! Every day!" We briefly revisited the replaying tape of negative messages from her childhood that became triggered when she felt the chaos starting to escalate. Being a "PK" (pastor's kid) was a mix of hard and good. She loved that she had a rich foundation of faith instilled at a young age, but she did not like the pressure always to be the "good kid." Even though her father was a biblical rock, she often felt she was second or third to the congregation. When her daughter was screaming about her clothes, her smoke detector alerted her that danger was looming. Her dream when she was running down the hall trying to figure out which door to open to get to her children ignited a similar trapped feeling that her daughter felt in the itchy shirt. I gently invited Brooke to consider, "You don't have to keep running to find the right door." Mark held her hand, and they both took deep breaths.

Understanding the three P's can bring clarity and empower us to slow down the juggling act in our home's circus.

Prepare

Proverbs 21:5 states, "The plans of the diligent lead to profit as surely as haste leads to poverty," This is also directly related to being fully seen, which creates safety in our brains. Preparing for the "battle" of the witching hour between school and dinnertime or a long Saturday at home with the kids will be a gift to all. Brooke and Mark learned to prepare ahead for the difficult mornings by having their daughter choose her outfit between three options the night before.

The preparation for the evening starts with the parents during the day. Remember, Sally used her ten-minute drive to school to prepare for the mix of emotions that would be entering her car after picking up her children from school. Mark and I worked separately for some sessions to utilize strategies to help with his ADHD brain. Brooke began to take walks in the mornings when the children were at school to ground herself. Parents can help their children choose healthy regulation by being prepared with emoji charts to help name their feelings. Agreed-upon signals can help couples and parents strengthen their connection. I also taught Mark and Brooke to text each other with an agreed-upon emoji to give each other a heads-up of the home's energy. Then, Mark would know Brooke needed an extra act of service to fill her bucket. Brooke would encourage and affirm Mark with her words. Preparing is diligently arming ourselves to choose to connect with God, within, and with others.

Preparing is diligently arming ourselves to choose to connect with God, within, and with others.

Prioritize

First Corinthians 6:19–20 encourages us to prioritize self-care because our "bodies are the temple of the Holy Spirit" (NMB). As parents, we can learn to sprinkle in taking care of ourselves during the day. Yes, we all would love a spa day, but that is not always possible. Modeling self-care will show your children simple ways they can also connect within themselves. Some examples include walking around your office for ten minutes, taking five deep breaths when you are on the way to pick up your children, taking three photos out in nature that match your feelings, or talking to a trusted friend for a few minutes.

Perspective

Parenting from a whole-brain perspective is life-giving. A child's prefrontal cortex is not fully developed until the mid-twenties. This does not mean they get a free pass to be disrespectful while they are having an almond tantrum, but it helps us understand that they don't have all the circuitry to react logically and balance their big feelings. Parents, we don't have to buy the most expensive leggings or give the second cookie, but as you're saying no for the thousandth time, monitor your triggers by pausing to remember that these requests are related to a lack of prefrontal cortex development. From the child's perspective, they must be "on" all day; they are exhausted when they get home from school. As adults, we get to choose when to exit a room and go to the bathroom, for example. But a child in a traditional school setting has to wait and ask permission anytime they want to leave the classroom. Having a whole-brain perspective (recognizing that our children's brain systems are overwhelmed after a day of performing at school) will reduce the pressure a child feels at home, which will empower all to have a balanced connection.

Letting Go to Be Able to Balance

Mindfulness can help us let go of the traps we find ourselves in. One powerful tool is using bubble meditation. I like to softly close my eyes and imagine I am walking toward the ocean. As I walk, my feet touch the warm sand. I hear the seagulls. I see the glistening sea. I smell the salt air. I taste the salty spray from the waves. As I am walking, I imagine holding a bubble into which I have put all my worries. The bubble is wiggly in my hands as I approach the shore. I raise my hands as if to reach up and let go of the bubble. It begins to bounce up and float above the sparkly water. I imagine God's hands gently reaching down to hold the bubble for me. For a while, I sense a lightness, and I let go and feel a balance of connection with God within my soul, heart, and mind. When I am ready, I open my eyes.

Feather for Your Day

First Peter 5: 6–7 states, "So humble yourselves under the mighty power of God, and at the right time he will lift you up in honor. Give all your worries and cares to God, for he cares about you" (NLT).

—Tricia Thornton—

Journal and Reflection Questions

For Discussion

Can you identify any false selves? When do you feel they started?

_____

_____

_____

_____

What do you feel holds you back from embracing balance?

_____

_____

_____

_____

How do the three P's play out in your life? Is there one that is more
 difficult than the others?

_____

_____

_____

_____

A Verse for Balance

"I press on to reach the end of the race and receive
the heavenly prize for which God, through Christ
Jesus, is calling us."

Philippians 3:14 NLT

Part 7
Embrace

God hugs you. You are encircled by the arms of the mystery of God.

—Saint Hildegard of Bingen

One who gets wisdom loves his soul. One who treasures understanding prospers.

—Proverbs 19:8 TLV

Chapter 19

The Searching Life of Elizabeth

"It is a beautiful day! Today, I'm going to spend time walking and planning!" Elizabeth has just returned from her church's women's retreat. She's feeling energized and has a cup full of ideas. She's always wanted to open a flower shop, but life keeps getting in the way. As she is walking by the lake, her mind gets pulled away. *How does she do it? How does my leader really keep it all balanced? I bet she's really not doing well on the inside. She and her husband can't really be that connected.*

A bird calls out as squirrels rustle in the leaves, and quickly she regains some presence. *Ugh, why do I always compare myself? I am a great mom, wife, and daughter of God! Stop it!* She hurries for the rest of the walk because she needs to get back for a Zoom call with her daughter to discuss wedding flowers. *I am so excited! I wonder if the flowers will be as pretty as the ones from Lisa's daughter's wedding?*

—Tricia Thornton—   159

Before she gets on the call, she decides to get some ideas by flipping through her wedding album from her special day twenty-eight years ago. She feels a tug toward sadness as she remembers her life at twenty-three. She was in the throes of fighting a battle with an eating disorder. Her husband, close friends, and family knew, but she still remembers the lonely feelings.

She tries to sit on the couch to do the connect-with-the-heart activity she learned in therapy. *Maybe I should call Tricia and go back in before the wedding? Yeah right, when will I fit that in? Plus we cannot have any other expenses right now. This wedding is not cheap!*

Ding! The reminder on her phone alerts her she has five minutes before the Zoom call. One more glance at the album, and she shuts it as if to say "Move on!" After the call, she goes into do-it mode. Her son is flying in from Boston next week. She goes into his room still decorated with camo and all her son's soccer posters. She pauses and feels frozen in time. She laughs. *I better pick up all these house plans and magazine cutouts. The kitchen remodel is on hold anyway.* Time has blown by, and it is time for her to run to her painting class.

Chapter 20

The Comparison Loop of Embrace

At the beginning of my two-and-a-half-year journey of writing *Blessing From Fear*, I discovered a box of some of my childhood journals. As I sat and read through them, I would laugh, weep, and shudder at the mixed feelings I carried during elementary through high school. I was often on a treadmill of *doing*, and then I would get knocked into comparison loops. Later in adolescence, my writing gave me glimpses into how I would emotionally bypass the fearful feelings and flee into a life of *doing*. I believe that my can-do spirit served me well. My "Little Engine That Could" energy persevered when my guidance counselor told me I could not get into Vanderbilt University. My doing self sometimes would overpower my True Self. I often would allow busyness to guide my life rather than turn to God for guidance. I constantly was filling my head with distractions, for if I slowed down, I would feel the fear rise, and that was too scary. In my journals, it was evident that I became trapped by comparison. The negative ideas of what others thought of me overpowered my ability to embrace the love and true acceptance of myself and, ultimately, of God.

The Swirls of Comparison Loops

Many books are written and podcasts recorded about the dangers of comparison loops. It is undoubtedly a pertinent subject, because in the digital world and the twenty-four-hour news society we live in, it is too easy to get caught in the trap of comparison. Galatians 6:4–5 implores, "Each one should test his own actions. Then they can take pride in themselves alone, without comparing themselves to someone else, for each one should carry their own load." I have found three steps that are very helpful as we attempt to retreat from the swirls of comparison loops.

Recognize the Feeling Spiral

Most of our characters in this book, and maybe even me and you, experience actual or perceived fear. As we have learned, the amygdala wakes up in this moment, which elicits a physical response from us. As that reaction occurs, we experience many big feelings, causing a variety of emotions. We now know several ways to name our feelings, activate our vagus nerve, and embrace balance. We will go from feeling powerless to powerful. Hence, we are empowered to authentically connect to the here and now, lessening the swirling sting of comparison.

Capture the Thoughts

Part of getting out of the loop happens when we seize the overwhelming thoughts. Remember QZE. We want to focus on positive versus negative in order to release the hold of anxious thoughts. By capturing the thoughts of comparison, we are rewiring our neuroplastic brains. Then, we wield an inner strength to fight the battle of the spirals.

Shift to an Attitude of Gratitude

After years of trying to go over or around the valleys in my life, I changed my attitude toward going *through* the hard times with a mindset shift. Romans 12:2 encourages that we have the power of choice. Proverbs 2:1–8 reassures us that we have the power through the knowledge of God to turn our ears to wisdom. Gratitude does not mean you are okay with tragic pain, but it allows you to be thankful that God gives you the strength to endure trials. Gratitude shifts us to be powerful versus powerless in the comparison loops.

—Tricia Thornton—

The Brain's Role in Embrace

Neuroanatomist Dr. Jill Bolte Taylor, in her profound book *Whole Brain Living*, discusses her extensive research of the anatomy of our brains. After enduring and recovering from a stroke, her research, backed by personal experience, states, "We have the power to turn our emotional circuitry on and off by choice."[18] Dr. Taylor has documented that our emotions take ninety seconds to be flushed through our bloodstream. As we have discussed, your senses send your brain a message that it receives into your thalamus. When you have an emotional response, it will take that reaction ninety seconds to go through your system. So, I like to think that I have a minute and a half to choose to embrace the present moment or go down the feeling spiral toward powerlessness. To embrace the here-and-now moment, choose activities that fit with your lifestyle. Some suggestions are to take a walk and notice nature around you; activate the vagus nerve through breathwork; create with a form of expressive arts; engage the five senses by asking yourself what you see, hear, touch, smell, and taste; and use the hand on your heart activity and name your feelings that you feel in the present moment.

Spiritual Insights of Embrace

We all have seen the heartwarming videos of soldiers returning from deployment to the warm embrace of loved ones. I also feel a hug daily as I walk into the house to my white German shepherd, ready to accept a pet and a hug. We watch athletes ecstatically tackling one another in celebration and joy after winning a big game. I imagine an authentic embrace when I read about the father running out to welcome home his wayward son in the parable in Luke 15.

Henri Nouwen inspired me through his book *The Return of the Prodigal Son*, in which he encourages us to keep our eyes peeled toward Home. The three characters in the titular parable, the younger son, the elder son, and the father, all go through their own journey toward embracing the heavenly Father's love. Luke 15:20 recounts, "So he got up and went to his father. But while he was a long way off, his father saw him and was filled with compassion for him; he ran to his son, threw his arms around him and kissed him."

Feather for Your Day

2 Corinthians 10:5 encourages us to "take captive every thought to make it obedient to Christ."

Chapter 21
Discovering the Truths
Versus Lies to Embrace

Elizabeth entered my therapy room with a spring in her step while holding a photo album. I was excited to see her, for it had been about a year since she was last in my office. The wedding was over, and she had a few photos printed at the drugstore to remember the special day. She laughed and said, "You know me, I want the pics from the photographer to be perfect, so these are just a few for me to show my close friends."

I genuinely enjoyed seeing all the beautiful smiles, and the flowers were gorgeous. After settling in, I looked at her and gently asked, "What would help you most today?"

She answered with an empty stare. "I don't know."

I reassured her and said, "That's completely okay; let's discover it together." We started by catching up about the children and how she and her husband were adjusting to being empty nesters. We landed on the truth that even though her chicks had flown from the nest, she and her husband felt quite full. Then, I noticed a soft tear well up. "Elizabeth, if that tear could talk, what would it be saying?"

She swallowed and said, "Thank you. I have missed our connection." I teared up, too, and we continued on to explore the direction to go.

"How about we review where we left off and where your journey has taken you over the past year." She nodded in affirmation. We began.

Truth Versus Lies

All through Scripture, we read how individuals and groups go toward God, away from God, and back again. Especially all through the Old Testament, we witness these back-and-forth journeys. One truth woven throughout is that God's love, omnipotence, and grace, is always present. Even in dark trials, God's embrace never ceases to direct His children how to discern truth from lies.

I often help clients name the truths and lies in their minds to ground them back to the present moment. This is essential in trauma recovery work. What is vital to uncovering truths is to have self-compassion. Sometimes, the road to embracing truths can take time, for we may have to peel away layers to see our core God images. Our inner critics can distract us with lies and block us from being gentle with ourselves. Having self-gentleness is the key to embracing God's steadfast love. Learning to parent ourselves gently frees us to authentically parent our children with love. Let's discover some tools that will help us learn how to embrace.

Learning to parent ourselves gently frees us to authentically parent our children with love.

Tools to Use to Embrace

Elizabeth decided to come back to therapy weekly for a little while. She felt she was on the verge of a new life of compassionately embracing herself. We discussed how she felt disjointed through her younger years, early in her marriage and motherhood. I could relate to her. She felt like a caterpillar who had spun a cocoon. She had been in a season of passively waiting, and now she was actively

Feather for Your Day

Moses felt doubt when he was called by God to lead the Israelites into the Promised Land. He kept his eyes on the Lord even though he did not feel he was strong or smart enough for the job. God reassured him in Exodus 3:12, "I will be with you. And this will be the sign to you that it is I who have sent you: When you have brought the people out of Egypt, you will worship God on this mountain."

—Tricia Thornton—

waiting as she was starting to fully see herself and God. Soon, she and I were discovering where her newfound butterfly wings would take her. We reviewed some tools to remind her of the everlasting embrace of God and how she could embrace herself and others.

Shelf Activity

Once we capture intrusive and overwhelming thoughts, we may become stuck with what to do with them. It's similar to when I told Francine that thoughts are like floating files on a computer. We need a place to land the file. The shelf activity helps us categorize the barrage of lies from our inner critics. With my clients, I often visually discuss this activity. For children, I may use a dragon; for adults, I might use a dark rock to represent negative thoughts (or the replay of a traumatic event). I will hold the object on top of my head and say, "Here is the bad dream or the scary memory or the betrayal you experienced. Let's imagine taking it out of your brain and putting it on a shelf." I will then point out it's like our brains are open and a little empty. Sometimes, I'll even place an empty bowl or cup on my head. I will explain that when we take out a negative thought, we must replace it with a positive one. So, I then put a shiny crystal stone on my head to show that we have now put a truth into our brains. The shelf activity demonstrates the power we have to choose what to put on the shelf and when to take it off, leading us to begin to gently embrace. To embrace this power that we can choose what and when to retrieve off the shelf can lead to a renewed sense of freedom.

—Beyond Blessed Parenting—

Expressive Arts

We have talked about the power of naming our feelings through-out this book. Using creative ways to focus on our feelings can be a life-giving embrace toward connection. But sometimes we get stuck in our heads when we are trying to name our feelings. The following questions are helpful for adults and children when the words are not surfacing. Sometimes, I will have a client draw while I ask these questions; sometimes, they will talk it out:

- What color is the feeling?
- Is it a straight, curvy, wavy, or jagged line?
- Is it a particular shape?
- Is it smooth, rough, or sharp?
- Is it wet or dry?

This activity will open the brain to the present moment so we can journey toward an inner embrace.

Brainy Tidbit

Imagery allows the emotional center to be activated. Once it is woken up, we can choose a healthy action to offer connection.

Having Gumption to Embrace

Are you familiar with the rom-com film *The Holiday*? One of my favorite scenes is when Kate Winslet's character is surprised by an unannounced visit from her toxic on-again, off-again boyfriend. After seeing him and realizing she does not want to be with him any longer, she slams the door, turns with her hands in the air, and squeals with freedom. She describes the feeling as having gumption. Embracing God and our True Selves is the doorway to the cross of connection. It takes gumption and courage to trust that "God is greater than our feelings, and he knows everything."[19]

Embracing God and our True Selves is the doorway to the cross of connection.

Feather for Your Day

On one of Paul's journeys to Rome, he reassured believers, "But now I urge you to keep up your courage, because not one of you will be lost; only the ship will be destroyed" (Acts 27:22).

Journal and Reflection Questions

For Discussion

What thoughts tend to jump-start your comparison trap to begin?

_____

_____

_____

_____

What lies come rushing in that cover up the truths in your life?

_____

_____

_____

_____

What can you choose to put on the shelf for the time being to embrace connection with God, within yourself, with another, and with your children?

_____

_____

_____

_____

A Verse for Embrace

"For we are God's masterpiece. He has created us anew in Christ Jesus, so we can do the good things he planned for us long ago."

Ephesians 2:10 NLT

Conclusion

You will never understand who you are until you understand who God is.

—Billy Graham, *The Journey*

I do know without a doubt we are all beautiful children of God that have been given a strong, resilient whole body from our brilliant brains to our nimble toes.

—Tricia Thornton, *Blessing From Fear*

I see and hear you are having some feelings. I wonder if there is a way we could figure this out together? I may not know you personally, but I have looked into the eyes of many parents to see pain, fear, loss, joy, confusion, angst, panic, relief, exhaustion, and acceptance. Without a doubt, we can all conclude that parenting is not easy. It is a trying road of twists and turns with many hills and valleys. Sometimes, we can't imagine loving our children any more than we do, yet we also often worry as we search for the right way to parent them. Do we really believe that parenting is not about perfection but about connection? We desire with every fragment of our souls to protect and love them, yet the shadows of our past and present pull us away. Parenting ourselves first requires us to receive grace from our heavenly parent.

Parenting is a battlefield, and Ephesians 6:10–18 describes how we can put on the armor of God. Battles are scary and are full of unknowns. When we choose to arm ourselves, we can better embrace the cross of connection. "Therefore, put on every piece of God's armor so you will be able to resist the enemy in the time of evil. Then after the battle you will still be standing firm" (Ephesians 6:13 NLT). All seven of the principles in this book are achievable because God designed our brains to be able to instill them. We can silence the noise to listen to His Word with God's guidance. We can acknowledge His power and holiness to renew our weary souls. We can accept God's forgiveness so we can balance the barrage of fear to forgive. Then we can embrace all parts of ourselves to connect with God, within ourselves, and with others.

—Tricia Thornton—

Often, a movie will end, and we wonder what happened next. Sometimes we want an ending that is all tied up neatly with a bow. Each of the characters in this book still struggled as they continued through life, but they all began to feel a sense of healing as they embraced authentic connection. Let's see where our new friends we have gotten to know in these pages are now in their next chapter.

Sally has been able to add moments of silence into her day. She has felt a new sense of stillness. Her Martha-like busy brain still fills her head with noise as she parents her four children, but she is learning the importance of balance. When her fawn response activates, she's courageously able to actively wait for God's direction.

Lawson continues to learn to listen to God as well as the cues from his five senses, his wife, and his children. He and his wife come back to therapy for regular check-in sessions. He has started going to a yoga class and can notice what his body is telling him, especially when his insecure attachment style surfaces. He is most excited about planning a future trip to the United States Open Championship golf tournament.

Alexander's daughters are now in college. He has been enjoying more time acknowledging all parts of himself, even when he feels like freezing or fleeing. He has been learning to prioritize time to journal in various ways. He discovered an old camera of his father's and has enjoyed dabbling with photography. He had begun to feel a sense of closeness to his deceased father that he had not felt before. He regularly sends texts to his young adult children full of affirming language. He has had great delight in setting up a foundation to provide scholarships in honor of his late coach.

Rose has been enjoying her grandchildren's activities. She has been paying close attention to when her fawn response is activated while balancing her time with her church groups. She is excited to welcome her youngest daughter's first child in a few months. She and her oldest daughter have come in for a few sessions together as they develop healthy boundaries and continue to move through the trauma continuum. The memories from the traumatic event are a part of Rose's story. She has been able to start to find meaning by leading a group at her church for other grandparents who have experienced trauma. She recently sent me a picture of all the family standing outside the newly constructed memorial in honor of the gas station tragedy. Even with the pain, she has begun to sense a renewed spirit from God's grace.

Francine, now in her early fifties, has begun to embrace her empty-nest chapter. She recently started dating a gentleman and has enjoyed discovering their love languages. She has been regularly visiting her girls in college, and they still use some of the same signals to help when their fight responses come online. She started taking walks with two other women who experienced abuse as children. Their rich conversations have enlightened her to continue exploring the idea of forgiveness.

Brooke's children are both in school more days. She has started to embrace balance more as she and Mark prepare for the rushed mornings and weekends. She is prioritizing self-care by continuing her morning routine of nature walks. She has started back to work part-time and is learning to balance her busy days. Her son's health is doing well. She now uses the knowledge she acquired about the heart condition to help a coworker whose daughter is having some of the same issues. Brooke continues to recognize better the triggers she feels when her husband's ADHD brain becomes overwhelming.

Elizabeth has been planning a birthday girls' trip. They are going to enjoy a tour of museums to celebrate her love of the arts. Her love of painting has continued to strengthen her faith. When she feels frozen from worry, she has learned to put on the shelf the rush of anxiety. She feels power when she decides when to retrieve it to embrace her fears with harmony. She still dreams of opening a flower shop, but for now, she is over the moon about her daughter expecting her first child. Embracing multiple feelings simultaneously has shown her that she can choose to connect with God even when she is not sure of the exact path ahead.

I have accepted the following truth through writing, my personal faith journey, parenting myself and my girls, my marriage, and my work as a speaker and therapist: Vulnerability is a strength. Counter to what we may have been taught, it is through emptiness that we will become full. "My grace is all you need. My power works best in weakness" (2 Corinthians 12:9 NLT). With God's power, we can break down the walls of fear and embrace all the blessings of parenthood.

With all our tools in our toolbox and armed with God's grace, we can face the battles. There will be moments and seasons when we feel the load and losses are too much to bear. Within our whole hearts, souls, and minds, we can courageously kneel at the cross and connect with God, within ourselves, with another, and with our children. Let's invite Jesus's words to wash over us: "Take my yoke upon you and learn from me, for I am gentle and humble in heart, and you will find rest for your souls" (Matthew 11:29).

Author's Notes

I am amazed that writing this book was not as cumbersome as writing my first one. It took less than half the time, which was a bummer because I always cherish my solo writing retreats. There are a few reasons why this book flowed with ease. First, it is what I do all day as a therapist as I walk alongside tired and anxious parents. Second, I have personally learned the hard way what happens when we don't prioritize parental self-care. Third, I have become passionate about spreading this message about authentic connection. It is integral to our children, our marriages, and all of us as parents.

As a young parent of two children, I remember too many times laying my head down at night and feeling disconnected from God, myself, and others. I remember often thinking, *Is this it?* I thought parenting would be joyful instead of being riddled with fear. Certainly, I still experience angst, fear, and uncertainty, but

I have learned how to face the challenges from a more connected place. I know all too well that parenting is not about perfection but about connection.

Do I fully embrace all seven of the principles? No, not without a struggle. Does the world's noise fill my head and not allow me to experience silence? Yes. Do I struggle with not being able to be still enough to listen? Yes. Do I sometimes feel paralyzed by fear and feel blocked from acknowledging my feelings and the goodness of God? Yes. Does busyness weaken my Hula-Hoop boundaries, causing me not to feel renewed strength? Yes. To protect myself, do I become rigid and allow myself to become the focus and not accept forgiveness? Yes. Do I feel pulled in all directions, causing me to feel anything but balanced? Yes. Does embracing gratitude and God's plan feel overwhelming some days? Yes.

Even if we read every parenting book, listen to the best podcasts, take the right supplements, and use every tool from this book, we will still feel the mountains and valleys of parenting. Without a doubt, I now know that by choosing to take care of myself and turn my eyes and ears to God, I can be a more present and empowering parent. The inner battle is real. Our flesh desires to do it one way, and our Spirit-led Self longs for freedom. The civil war within can be faced through us laying down the fight at the feet of God. I have personally chosen and watched many clients choose to strengthen their connection with God and themselves and then be able to experience authentic connection with others.

When you feel weary and don't feel like taking care of yourself, pause and use your five senses to come to the present moment.

The current state may be scary, but we know that tomorrow has enough worry. As Moses encouraged Aaron to bless the Israelites, "The LORD bless you and keep you" (Numbers 6:24). Let's walk forward together, and I eagerly await to meet you again.

Endnotes

1. Tricia Thornton, *Blessing From Fear* (Fitting Words, 2024), 9.

2. Kendra Cherry, "4 Types of Attachment Styles," Verywell Mind, last modified December 14, 2023, https://www.verywellmind.com/attachment-styles-2795344.

3. Thornton, *Blessing From Fear*, 207.

4. C. S. Lewis, *A Grief Observed* (HarperCollins, 1961), 1.

5. Jenna Riemersma, *Altogether You: Experiencing Personal and Spiritual Transformation with Internal Family Systems Therapy* (Pivotal Press, 2020), 4.

6. *The Whole-Brain Child: 12 Revolutionary Strategies to Nurture Your Child's Developing Mind* (Bantam Books, 2012), 43.

7. Leaf, *Switch on Your Brain*, 108.

8. Thornton, *Blessing From Fear*, 205.

9. Tara-Leigh Cobble, "Day 353 (Titus 1–3)," posted December 18,

2023, by the Bible Recap, YouTube, 3:18, https://www.youtube.com/watch?v=g6Ld_P6fK74&ab_channel=TheBibleRecap.

10. Chapter 21 of *Blessing From Fear* is dedicated to the 5 Love Languages. You can check it out for a more in-depth look at the subject.

11. For additional resources, visit Dr. Gary Chapman's website: "What Are the 5 Love Languages?" Love Languages, accessed May 14, 2025, https://5lovelanguages.com/learn.

12. David Kessler, *Finding Meaning: The Sixth Stage of Grief* (Scribner, 2019), 70.

13. Caroline Leaf, *Switch on Your Brain*, 60.

14. Matthew 6:34 NIV.

15. You can read more about the "Little Girl with a Curl" and "Chicken Little" false selves in Sue Monk Kidd, "From False Self to True Self," chapter 3 in *When the Heart Waits: Spiritual Direction for Life's Sacred Questions* (HarperCollins, 2006).

16. Kidd, *When the Heart Waits*, 59.

17. Jill Bolte Taylor, *Whole Brain Living: The Anatomy of Choice and the Four Characters That Drive Our Life* (Hay House, 2021), 6.

18. Leaf, *Switch on Your Brain*, 75

19. 1 John 3:20 NLT.